PRODUCTION, DISTRIBUTION, AND GROWTH IN TRANSITIONAL ECONOMIES

Praeger Series in Political Economy
Rodney Green, *Series Editor*

PRODUCTION, DISTRIBUTION, AND GROWTH IN TRANSITIONAL ECONOMIES

M. Katherine Perkins

Foreword by Keith Hart

PRAEGER

New York
Westport, Connecticut
London

Library of Congress Cataloging-in-Publication Data
Perkins, M. Katherine.
  Production, distribution, and growth in transitional
economies.

  (Praeger series in political economy)
  Bibliography: p.
  Includes index.
  1. Economic development. 2. Production (Economic
theory) 3. Distribution (Economic theory)
4. Dependency. I. Title. II. Series.
HD75.P47 1988   338.9   87-29292
ISBN 0-275-92104-2 (alk. paper)

Library of Congress Catalog Card Number: 87-29292

ISBN: 0-275-92104-2

First published in 1988

Praeger Publishers, One Madison Avenue, New York, NY 10010
A division of Greenwood Press, Inc.

Printed in the United States of America

The paper used in this book complies with the
Permanent Paper Standard issued by the National
Information Standards Organization (Z39.48-1984).

10 9 8 7 6 5 4 3 2 1

This book is dedicated to
Jeffrey Lee Colvin
My loving husband and best friend

CONTENTS

FOREWORD by KEITH HART

Mary Katherine Perkins is an American political economist who has worked mainly on the development problems of Latin America and the Caribbean. During the postwar period a broad consensus emerged in Latin America, at least in political circles left of center, on the causes of underdevelopment and its remedies. This consensus was opposed to the prevailing orthodoxy of the 1950s and 60s, "modernization theory," according to which the sustained failure of many Third World countries to make the transition to an advanced level of industrial capitalism was attributed to the intrinsic backwardness of their societies and cultures. In the view of many American social scientists, "modernization" required the replacement of traditional institutions by an idealized package that was thought to have served the western bourgeoisie well in its drive towards capitalism: a combination of cities, entrepreneurship, scientific technology, education, law, democracy, and a set of cultural values compatible with rational individualism.

Not surprisingly, this diagnosis was rejected by many Latin American thinkers, of whom André Gunder Frank was the most prominent. According to them, the problem facing Third World economies was not the relative absence of capitalism, but rather the distortions introduced by its active presence in these regions. Poor countries had for a long time been restructured through integration into a world economy dominated by foreign capitalist powers. Their underdevelopment, far from being a pristine condition, was the result of dependent incorporation into a global process of capital accumulation. Surpluses were extracted from Third World economies by means of national and international structures that effectively blocked their chances of autonomous development. The reproduction of these structures was the ongoing cause of underdevelopment. The only escape route was some kind of socialist transformation outside the world capitalist economy.

This intellectual position, sometimes known as the "development of underdevelopment" school, received widespread currency in the Third World from the 1960s onwards, being taken up most notably by George Beckford and the "plantation" school of Caribbean political economists, and by Samir Amin, whose corpus of writings constitutes the most general statement along these lines. The debt crisis of the 1980s has done nothing to weaken such arguments, as country after country falls into the clutches of the IMF in consequence of chronic failure to meet their interest payment obligations and foreign trade bills. The overall outlook for Third World development seems bleak at this time, and indigenous intellectuals might be excused for supposing that the "world system" precludes substantial economic progress on the part of poor countries.

During the last two centuries similar theories of underdevelopment, advocating partial withdrawal behind protectionist barriers, have been popular in countries facing the awesome task of competing with the more advanced industrial economies—first Britain, then North America, Europe, and Japan. Alexander Hamilton and Andrew Jackson promoted protection for the infant manufacturing industries of the United States and Friedrich List's "National System of Political Economy" (1841) inspired German and Central European attempts to develop from an initially backward position. The fact is that the world system of capitalism has never been closed or monolithic, as is attested by the successful economic transformation of many small peripheral European nations at an earlier period, and by the rise of the Southeast Asian NICs today. If little Finland, in its exposed strategic situation, can develop in less than 100 years from being a Swedish colony and Russian protectorate to the position of having the ninth highest GNP per capita in the world (World Bank Development Report 1987), in what sense can it be said that global capitalism blocks development in the periphery?

Underdevelopment theory has also been severely criticized from within the Marxist discourse to which it has normally claimed an affiliation. Some writers (for example, Robert Brenner) have claimed that Frank's emphasis on structures of trade and finance neglects the focus on production that was always essential to the approach advocated by Marx and Lenin. In general, there does seem to have been only restricted intellectual interchange between the New and Old Worlds in such matters. One feature of twentieth century social science has been the extreme fragmentation of discourse into separate national, regional, and linguistic compartments. A vigorous debate on the historical origins of capitalism in England (see Hilton 1976) and a revival of Marxist social theory in Paris around the leading figure of Louis Althusser do not seem to have made much impact on the theories of economic development now current in Latin America and the Caribbean. As a result, the possibility of new syntheses emerging has been seriously impeded, and the tired litany of oppression by the United States has been allowed to continue largely unchallenged as the principal explanation for the region's underdevelopment.

Katherine Perkins has set out explicitly to remedy this situation. She is remarkably familiar with the arguments and circumstances of Latin America and the Caribbean. Yet she has also chosen to take seriously intellectual currents emanating from elsewhere. In particular, she develops a critique of underdevelopment theory from a standpoint that owes much to the French Structuralist Marxism of Althusser's followers,* while demonstrating considerable knowledge of Anglo-American Marxist economic history and theory. Such a line of inquiry depends on an unusual combination of linguistic and scholarly aptitudes; and these she possesses in full measure, being a fluent reader of English, French, and Spanish texts, as well as having spent prolonged periods outside her native USA, in Paris and the Caribbean.

Katherine Perkins, like many others before her, was first drawn to examining the chronic problem of inflation and debt in the economies of her chosen region. But, in seeking an appropriate explanatory framework, she was forced to extend the scope of her theoretical critique. The result is this book, which brings together the critical and constructive elements of a new approach to underdevelopment. Theories of economic development reflect much broader differences in epistemology, and Perkins has not avoided confronting such issues here. Consequently, her arguments are mainly abstract, and the concrete application of her approach to the economic history of Latin America and the Caribbean awaits a further volume now in preparation (*The Caribbean and Latin America in Transition*).

The organization of the present volume is as follows. In Chapters 2 and 3 the theory of underdevelopment now current in Latin America is opposed by a general introduction to French Structuralism, specifically to its Marxist variant. Chapters 4–7 introduce several key elements of Structuralist Marxism relevant to the theory of underdevelopment. Here a crucial distinction is drawn between synchronic and diachronic approaches, the first being a static theoretical abstraction of the capitalist

---

*It is one measure of the insularity of modern social science discourse that the term "Structuralism" generally refers in the New World, especially among economists, to the development approach associated with ECLA and Raul Prebisch in the 1950s; whereas in Europe it is taken to be a mainly French school of thought, drawing inspiration from Saussurian linguistics and introduced into Marxism by Althusser, Poulantzas and others in the 1960s. Katherine Perkins normally uses the expression in the second sense, but is well familiar with the first.

economy, while the second incorporates historical development into its analytical structures. Chapters 8–12 lay out Perkins' own distinctive theoretical approach, which focuses on the divergent forms of economic calculation (profit/rent) in social formations transitional between precapitalist and capitalist economic organization.

The author's exegesis of her case is at all times comprehensive and lucid. Indeed, a major contribution of this book is that the clarity and simplicity of its summaries may convince some English-speaking and Hispanic readers of the instructive value of a French discourse they may previously have found rather obscure. Nevertheless, it may be worthwhile for me to highlight a few major points as a guide to the rich content of this treatise. These are:

1. The essence of her critique of underdevelopment theory.
2. Development as a transition, both from feudalism to capitalism and from capitalism to socialism.
3. The theory of economic calculation in transitional social formations.
4. The problem of theory and history, conceived of as an opposition between synchrony and diachrony.
5. The wider epistemological critique of empiricism contained in Structuralist notions of science and ideology.

THE CRITIQUE OF UNDERDEVELOPMENT THEORY

The aspiration of Latin American and Caribbean countries has been to achieve autonomous capitalist development. Postwar protectionist policies aimed at import-substituting industrialization have failed to emulate similar programs of emancipation from economic backwardness undertaken by the United States, Germany, Japan, and some lesser European nations at an earlier stage in the development of the world economy. Underdevelopment theory attributes this failure largely to external causes, of which Katherine Perkins identifies three main analytical components: monopoly, surplus transfer, and the international division of labor. She finds the treatment of Third World economies in this theory to be generally ahistorical and oversimplified, with its reductionist focus on the problems of monocrop export agriculture.

The emphasis on monopolistic control of international trade by foreign corporations, in her view, treats capitalism as a non-dynamic abstraction, by removing from analysis the element of restless competition that has always been central to its development. Surpluses have undoubtedly been transferred out of Third World regions as part of a global process of capital accumulation; but what prevents them from being reinvested in the periphery, if economic opportunities there are so profitable? Amin's recapitulation of Prebisch's economic arguments on the effects of specialization within the international division of labor, showing how inequalities are reproduced, only works as an explanatory theory if capitalist relations of production are dominant on both sides of the exchange; and this is clearly not the case in many Third World countries. In short, underdevelopment theory has failed to generate adequate economic arguments to support its a priori conclusions and thereby stands indicted of logical, historical, and political errors.

Katherine Perkins prefers to replace the previous focus on a coherent world economic system with an approach that can identify the interaction between capitalist and non-capitalist elements in social formations whose transitional nature is attested by the priority given to their development. She refuses to treat non-capitalist classes and structures of production as relatively undifferentiated aspects of global capitalist accumulation, seeing such a view as trade-centered and unnecessarily monolithic. Class struggles, forms of state, and the accumulation process in the Third World are all, in her perspective, significantly affected by retention of some control over the means of production on the part of peasants and landlords in most of these countries. The prime intellectual task, therefore, ought to be to comprehend how the transition to capitalism is modified by the persisting influence of precapitalist economic elements.

DEVELOPMENT AS A TRANSITION

It is remarkable that recent Marxist discussion of the problem of transition has bifurcated into two distinct objects of discourse. Anglo-Americans have focused on the traditional historical concern with the origins of capitalism in its European feudal past; whereas French Marxists have been more interested in assessing the claim of the Soviet Union to have made a successful transition to socialism. The key text in the first case was Maurice Dobb's *Studies in the Development of Capitalism* (1947), which spawned a debate over the relative priority of production relations and trade in the emergence of a fully-fledged British capitalism. American economist Paul Sweezy took up a position that is consistent with underdevelopment theory's emphasis on trade and with the analogous "world systems" approach of Immanuel Wallerstein. Most independent observers would award the spoils in this particular argument to those who, with Dobb, prefer to stress the organization of production in the orthodox tradition of Marxist-Leninist analysis.

In the second (Parisian) case, the protagonists were defined principally by the struggle, following the Sino-Soviet split in the 1960s, between Stalinists and Maoists for leadership of the French extreme left. Here again, the question of the Soviet Union's standing as a socialist or state-capitalist economy hinged on the relative emphasis given to production relations over distributive arrangements. The clearest anti-Stalinist position was taken by Charles Bettelheim (1970), who argued that socialization of the legal forms of property had done little to alter the fundamentally capitalist organization of production in the Soviet Union. For French Structuralists, therefore, the problem of capitalist transition had a predominantly future orientation; whereas Anglo-Americans seemed to be locked in debate over capitalism's empirical past. In both cases, the pervasive influence of Stalinism over twentieth century Marxist politics had an implicit effect on the positions taken by participants in theoretical debate. Katherine Perkins is, to my knowledge, the first person to synthesise the principal results of both debates and to apply these to the arena of Third World development. Whatever her degree of success in achieving a practicable synthesis, the mere attempt is pathbreaking.

ECONOMIC CALCULATION IN TRANSITIONAL SOCIAL FORMATIONS

Katherine Perkins singles out two French Structuralist followers of Althusser as guides to the theoretical problems inherent in the study of capitalist development: Etienne Balibar and Pierre-Philippe Rey. She believes that each is seriously flawed, but, in the spirit of constructive eclecticism, she has drawn positively on the example of each. Balibar's famous essay "On the basic concepts of historical materialism" (1968) starts from a conception of modes of production as a structured set of relations between producers, non-producers, and means of production. He resolves the problem of capitalism's antecedents by proposing a "transitional" mode of production between feudal and capitalist modes, namely the system of manufactures, i.e., the organization of handicrafts in factories. Perkins prefers to see transitional social formations as a combination of several modes of production. In this she receives support from the "articulation of modes of production" school, whose leading exponent is Rey, an anthropologist who compared precolonial and colonial Africa with the transition to capitalism in British history (Rey 1973).

Unlike Rey and Balibar, Perkins does not seek to identify an intermediate mode of production between feudal or, in the African case, "lineage" modes and capitalism (i.e., petty commodity production or the system of manufactures). Nor does she assume that one mode of production is necessarily dominant at a given point of time in a social formation's evolution. She rejects Rey's conclusion that the non-capitalist elements of Third World economies are always restructured to meet the needs of a dominant foreign capitalism. Indeed, for her, their development problems are often best seen as being caused by the continued dominance of local precapitalist classes both in the local accumulation process and in the arena of nation-state politics. If there is often an alliance between capitalist and precapitalist classes, as Rey argues, it cannot be assumed that the resulting structure is inevitably dominated by capitalist interests nor that its teleology is the transition to capitalism.

One reason for Marxist intellectuals to assert the dominance of capitalism (just as orthodox economists must assume the preeminence of markets) is the need to retain the theoretical guidelines of an internally consistent analytical construct, here Marx's idea of the "historical laws of motion of the capitalist mode of production," as a basis for understanding developing economies. This problem was first encountered by the great Marxist theories of Russian and German social democracy at the turn of the century, notably by Lenin and Kautsky, as they struggled with the application of Marx's theory of capitalism and proletarian revolution to regions dominated by backward agriculture. (See Hussain and Tribe 1981, "Marxism and the agrarian question.") It has plagued Marxist discourse on economic development ever since.

Being unable to locate in the literature a non-teleological theory of the transition to capitalism, Perkins turns to Bettelheim's analysis of the transition from capitalism to socialism, where it is frankly admitted that capitalist and non-capitalist elements of economic organization can coexist within a given social formation without either being necessarily dominant. In particular, Bettelheim focuses on the forms of economic calculation. Following Marx, capitalist production is organized around the extraction of surplus-value; but the extraction of surplus labor in feudal economies takes the form of rent; and planned socialist economies seek to substitute alternative distribution mechanisms to those of capitalist profit-making under conditions of market competition.

Perkins' innovation is to apply this approach to Third World economies conceived of as being doubly determined by feudal and capitalist forms of economic calculation (both rent and profit). Although she does not stress the point, this line is similar to the one adopted by David Ricardo in his classical formulation of political economy at the beginning of Britain's industrial revolution (1817). Just as then, now in regions like Latin America, the state provides an arena for class struggles in which opposed economic principles clash. Perkins makes no a priori judgment about the transition to socialism under such circumstances. But she firmly rejects any notion that the idea of a direct transition from capitalism to socialism provides an appropriate conceptual framework for the analysis of political options in such regions. The problem of inflation and debt in Latin America and the Caribbean is best approached, in her view, as the product of competing forms of economic calculation in social formations that are part feudal and part capitalist, without either side being assumed to be dominant in any given instance.

SYNCHRONY AND DIACHRONY

The problem of Third World economic development has mounted a systematic challenge to economic theory in this century. Both liberal and Marxist versions of the theory of market capitalism proceed by constructing a system of analytical identities on the basis of deductive axioms whose origins may be variably historical, but whose logical structures are effectively formal and static. Very few Marxists have been able to follow Lenin's model in taking a genuinely dialectical line on the evolution of Marx's concepts in history. One exception would be C.L.R. James (see "Notes on Dialectics" 1948). The majority seek to reproduce the master's formal categories or those generated by Lenin and Trotsky in the heat of the Russian revolution as an unreflecting and immobile foundation for understanding later developments. Such theoretical abstractions automatically pose gigantic problems when confronted with the task of explaining the "real world," especially when that world is represented as an evanescent process of becoming, of historical development, rather than as a mature and coherent economic structure. The issue of theory and history normally appears to English-speaking economists of both right and left as a task of approximation and modification of rationalist theorems in the light of more immediate empirical observations.

French Structuralists approach the dilemma in a different way, being guided by the epistemologies of Descartes and Kant rather than by a positivist tradition informed by the legacy of Galileo and Bacon. They conceive of analytical structures as being rational, not empirical in origin; and, following the great linguist, Ferdinand de Saussure, they distinguish between "synchronic" structures (which are abstracted from historical time altogether, much as the grammar of a language) and "diachronic" structures (which describe movement in an abstract version of time, e.g. historical semantics, but are not real history itself, i.e., concrete speech events).

Perkins takes up this Structuralist distinction to develop, in the middle chapters, a number of interesting technical discussions. First she considers the economics of capitalism as a synchronic system in isolation from the non-capitalist structures with which it is invariably associated in real historical time. She then introduces a diachronic approach to capitalism, which treats development or historical transition from a viewpoint that is still abstractly theoretical, but that admits of a plurality of structures. She rightly considers such a procedure to be essential to the construction of a coherent theory of the transition to capitalism or socialism, and she rigorously excludes reference to real historical processes that are often smuggled into discourse of this kind under the guise of ideal types such as "the Junker road to capitalism" or the "Asiatic mode of production." In other words, she separates the task of theory construction from that of historical description, even as she insists that a theory of economic development must rest both on a synchronic analysis of market capitalism and on a diachronic, non-teleological approach to economies combining capitalist and precapitalist elements.

SCIENCE VERSUS IDEOLOGY

The greatest obstacle to acceptance of Katherine Perkins' ideas in the English-speaking world (and its Hispanic counterpart) is that her epistemology is French. The proliferation of Marxism in the twentieth century has long ago removed any epistemological integrity from Marx's theoretical heritage. English and American Marxists have adapted their master's theories to an empiricist discourse appropriate to the societies in which they must function, increasingly as academics. Russian Marxism seems to most outsiders to be little more than a mystification of the exigencies of Stalin's rule. Third World Marxism is normally a nationalist response to foreign imperialism ("Yanqui go home"), while French Marxism usually appears more to non-Frenchmen as a brand of Parisian cafe intellectualism than as any other Marxism with which they are familiar.

Perkins has not shrunk from recognizing that her intellectual journey now sets her on a collision course with most of her colleagues in the economics profession. It is to be expected that orthodox economists would reject her analysis, but it is sad that most of her peers on the left, both in the United States and in the Third World, will find her approach at best unsympathetic, at worst incomprehensible. She documents clearly how the reception of Althusserian Structuralism by English-speaking Marxists has consistently been marred by epistemological confusion. The roots of this confusion lie in English and French cultural notions of what constitutes scientific knowledge. The terms "science" and "ideology" have been counterposed regularly in the modern era, indeed ever since organized religion ceased to command the support of most professional intellectuals. If "science" is a distinctively English notion and "ideology" an invention of the French—ever since Napoleon, and on both sides of the Channel, the normative construction of these paired terms has generally been to value "science" positively (true ideas) and "ideology" negatively (false ideas).

For English-speakers, scientific laws are derived from systematic observations of the real world. Ideas which cannot be clearly grounded in such observations are mere metaphysical speculation, "ideology." For French Structuralists, this anglophone construction of "science" is itself ideological. Following Continental philosophical traditions, they reject the possibility of deriving knowledge from natural observation, thereby making of "empiricism" a dirty word and linking it to a naive, egocentric "humanism" that refers all knowledge to individual experience. They hold that appearances offer no reliable guide to scientific determination of the world's phenomena. Rather, events on the surface can only be explained by reference to their inner essences. These "structures" are always and necessarily the product of rationalization by intellectuals: ordinary speakers of a language use its grammar unconsciously, but it takes a linguist to make explicit the rules underpinning its order. "Science" for them requires penetration beneath the level of appearances to structures revealed by the operation of reason. In this way Marx revealed the contradiction of the capital-labor relation as underlying the turmoil of modern markets.

Perkins believes that economic science should rest on the construction of rational theory (a belief she shares with orthodox microeconomic theorists such as Kenneth Arrow), and that most of her English-speaking and Hispanic colleagues are trapped in an ideological version of economics by their uninspected empiricist assumptions. In this interpretation, "science" is more or less synonymous with "good thinking," that is with "rationalism."

This variant of the ancient debate between Descartes and Bacon, between French rationalism and English empiricism, was transcended, in my opinion, by German idealism, by the dialectical philosophy of Kant and Hegel, which sought to place mind and its object in some active relationship. Certainly it was one of Althusser's aims to purge Marxism of its Hegelian antecedents and to bring Marxist science into line with the postwar avant-garde, with trans-Atlantic systems theory. Katherine Perkins likewise chooses to pitch her argument at a level that disputes the appropriate allocation of the positivist label "science" to the intellectual procedures adopted by political economists. Her rejection of dialectical reason, which seeks to relate appearances to essences in a more two-sided way, in favor of a French structuralism which some would judge to have had its day (hence the current vogue in literary salons for "post-Structuralism"), will not win her many friends either within or outside the circle of contemporary international Marxism.

Yet no reader of this volume can fail to be impressed by Perkins' intellectual rigor. Perhaps it is after all a major responsibility of economists, whether orthodox or Marxist, to introduce a measure of clear thinking into the hurly-burly of modern political economic discourse. It ought to be the case that her initiative would spark off a fresh appraisal of Althusserian theory in the English-speaking and Hispanic worlds. More likely, judgment will be postponed until the publication of her applied study of underdevelopment in Latin America and the Caribbean. In the meantime this book contains a pellucid and wide-ranging review of many fundamental issues that must be resolved if the analysis of development problems is to be placed on a sounder theoretical footing.

Keith Hart is an economic anthropologist from Cambridge University currently working as visiting professor at the Consortium Graduate School of Social Sciences, University of the West Indies, Mona, Jamaica. His work on West Africa (see "The Political Economy of West African Agriculture" 1982) led him to take an interest in the writings of French Marxists familiar with the same region, and thence to a broader epistemological engagement with Structuralist theory and its dialectical alternatives. He maintains a research focus on urbanization and migration in developing countries, and coined the expression "informal sector/ economy" in the early 1970s as an aspect of that research. He has taught at several North American and British universities.

ACKNOWLEDGMENTS

Throughout the writing of this book, I have had the considerable benefit of conversations with my husband, Dr. Jeff Colvin, on the theoretical issues raised by the book. I am forever indebted to him for his help, and, in fact, I doubt the writing could have proceded without it. I also received considerable support and guidance from my colleague at Howard, Dr. Rodney Green. I will remain grateful to him for his detailed comments on early and later drafts. I would also like to thank my other colleagues at Howard University, such as Professor Hilborne Watson, Chairman of the Political Science Department, and Dr. Cleveland Chandler, former Chairman of the Department of Economics. And I owe thanks to my research assistants at Howard, especially Herbert Ray Gilbert and Windell Thomas.

I made the final revisions of the manuscript during my stay at the University of the West Indies, and at the Institute for Social and Economic Research in Kingston, Jamaica. There, I received invaluable assistance from Professor Keith Hart of Cambridge University, who was a visiting professor at the Consortium Graduate School at UWI. He made numerous suggestions concerning the reorganization of the original draft; I am also indebted to Keith for writing the foreword to this book. Professor George Beckford, who was gracious enough to invite me to the University of the West Indies in the first place, also contributed many helpful comments, as well as much support and encouragement. Dr. Eddie Green very kindly opened to me the resources of the ISER, of which he is the Director. Among my other colleagues at UWI to whom I owe a debt of gratitude are: Richard Bernal, Omar Davis, Carl Stone, and

Michael Witter. I am grateful, as well, to my students at UWI for their penetrating questions and keen insights into the economics of "development"; I am certainly not the first academic scribbler to benefit from the immense fund of knowledge and understanding on this question that resides in the young minds of students in the developing world today.

I would like to thank all of my former professors, and especially E. J. Ford, Willi Semmler, and John Willoughby. Finally, I would like to thank those dear friends of mine whose support and encouragement meant so much to me: Robert Byrne, Sarah and Steve Sorkin, Tom Megan, Francine Pollack, and Dessima Williams.

1

INTRODUCTION

In recent years, impressive advances have been made in the theoretical treatment of the problem of underdevelopment. These advances are associated with the concept of the transition to capitalism in the underdeveloped world. However, despite an impressive number of applications of concepts such as the "articulation of modes of production," no thorough examination of the roots of this work has been attempted. It is the purpose of this book to argue for the application of theoretical work on transition to the problem of contemporary underdevelopment.

The first task is a careful statement of the problem. Toward this end, I examine theories of underdevelopment in Chapter 2. The Frank-Wallerstein approach, which dominates theories of underdevelopment, has recently been utilized by Banaji to explain rural incomes as "concealed wages." In Chapter 2, I criticize this theory, as well as its parent world system theory. It is my view that recent work in articulation of modes of production is an improvement in the formation of an approach to underdevelopment.

This recent work has several sources. It has philosophical roots in French Structuralism. Therefore, I introduce the reader to this school of thought in Chapter 3. After a general discussion of Louis Althusser, I move on to an analysis of the work of Etienne Balibar, Charles Bettelheim, and Pierre-Philippe Rey.

In Chapters 4 and 5, I turn to a more familiar subject, the capitalist mode of production, which is viewed in abstraction from the existence of noncapitalist social relations. Although much of the content of these chapters will be a review for the reader familiar with classical political economy, some new material on the deviation of prices from values is presented.

A social formation containing more than one mode of production is referred to as a diachrony. A more detailed discussion of theoretical diachrony begins in Chapter 6. Of extreme importance to the remainder of the book are the dislocations present in the concept of diachrony. These are taken up in Chapter 6. Chapter 7 considers Balibar's notion of a transitional mode of production. In this chapter I also attempt to answer the empiricist criticism of this concept as raised by Hindess and Hirst, and begin to develop a concept of transitional social formation. Chapters 8 and 9 subsequently take up concepts of dissimulation and economic calculation. All of these concepts will hopefully prove fruitful in helping us to understand the transition to capitalism in both Europe and in less developed countries.

A second focus for contemporary work on "modes of production" is the famous debate on the European transition from feudalism to capitalism. I discuss the existing theories about this transition in Chapter 10. Chapter 11 applies the insight gleaned from an analysis of these theories to the problem of economic calculation in different modes of production.

Finally, Chapter 12 returns to the issue of contemporary underdevelopment. I apply the concepts developed throughout the earlier chapters to (1) a general characterization of a developing country in transition, (2) the problem of internal and external economic relations, and (3) the role of prices in the accumulation of capital in a less developed country. In a future work, I will apply the theoretical framework developed in this volume to specific transitional economies in Latin America and the Caribbean.

2

THEORIES OF ECONOMIC DEVELOPMENT

The consequences of this differential determination of time, and of the distinction between the time of the dynamics and the time of history in general for the contemporary problem of *underdevelopment* (which is a favourite haunt for every theoretical confusion) cannot be expounded here; at least what we have said gives us a foretaste of its critical importance.[1]

The general thesis of this book is: questions concerning economic development can better be answered if we can define *development* in a more precise manner. In Latin America and the Caribbean, development has long been associated with the idea of modernization, but then we are left wondering what it means to be a modern economy and what must happen before a country can become modern. Such questions, however, have no definite answers. Another more precise notion of development has to do with the transition to capitalism. It is easier to gauge when a transition to capitalism has occurred, however roughly, than it is to say exactly when an economy has become modern, and we can then at least speculate on what would bring about such a transition. The concept is also less value-laden.

Before examining theories concerning the transition to capitalism, I shall briefly discuss theories of underdevelopment. Of greatest influence in Latin America and the Caribbean has been the "development of underdevelopment" theory. According to this well-known argument, associated with André Gunder Frank[2] and Immanuel Wallerstein,[3] whatever transition is to occur has taken place long ago, and furthermore, underdevelopment today is not a reflection of the failure of capitalist transition at all, but rather the *result* of the development of capitalism in the center.[4] Another important question that will be considered is whether social relations with a precapitalist character are a cause or an effect of underdevelopment. Finally, the "units of analysis" debate on the agrarian question is to be discussed, as this turns out to be, in many respects, a logical outgrowth of the "development of underdevelopment" argument.

THE DEVELOPMENT OF UNDERDEVELOPMENT

The theory of *development of underdevelopment* has its orgins in the structural theory of development formulated by the Economic Commission for Latin America (ECLA).[5] On the grounds that the terms of trade would inevitably turn against nations producing primary products, ECLA recommended that less developed countries (LDCs) protect key domestic industries whose growth would displace imports. When the central tenets of the ECLA theory were brought into question by the failure of import substitution industrialization in the mid 1950s, the "development of underdevelopment" school modified it without altering its most basic assumption: Latin American and Caribbean social formations are capitalist and, therefore, development of productive forces is automatic. When this development does not occur, it is due to external factors. The "development of underdevelopment" theory is thus closely related to the Latin American theory of dependency.

As several writers have pointed out, the principal contribution of the dependency theorists has been their description of a pattern of development different from that which has occurred in Europe and North America.[6]

The framework within which the ECLA model grew up involved, ironically, a strong belief in the potential for the autonomous growth of Latin American and Caribbean capitalism, a belief shared by both the International Monetary Fund (IMF) and ECLA. The question is: what blocks development? From the point of view of the IMF, the dynamism of Caribbean and Latin American economies is blocked by market distortions induced by inflation; from the ECLA perspective, it is held back by supply rigidities which, although domestic, are ultimately caused by forces external to domestic social formation.

The causal factors in the "development of underdevelopment" model are three: the international division of labor, monopoly, and the transfer of surplus. The pattern of specialization, forced upon the Caribbean and Latin America by rapid economic growth in Europe and North America, as well as by colonization, brought about the development of an export economy. One consequence of this is the special character of Caribbean and Latin American agriculture: it is primarily monocrop agriculture, in which output is increased by extending the land under cultivation.[7] Prior to 1930, the accessibility of uncultivated land compensated for the technical backwardness of export agriculture; moreover, the relatively slow-growing population was easily absorbed by the expansion of agriculture.[8] Following the world economic crisis of the 1930s, however, the growth potential of this type of cultivation was exhausted. The rising demand for food, stemming both from a rapid rate of growth in world population, and from urban industrial development, caused an increase in agricultural prices. In addition, the stagnation of agriculture resulted in rural unemployment and rural-to-urban migration.

In addition to rising demand for food, a second inflationary pressure, also caused by production for export, is a chronic tendency for import prices to rise. The Prebisch Thesis suggests that because of the type of commodity exported (food), the demand for the export would not rise in proportion to national income in the importing country; conversely, Caribbean and Latin American demand for exports from advanced capitalist countries would rise faster than national income since Caribbean and Latin American industrialization lead to greater demands for capital goods.[9] Consequently, even if the rate of growth in national income were the same for both countries, the Caribbean or Latin American trading partner would experience a transfer of surplus to the advanced capitalist country. This transfer would show up in a balance of payments crisis and in currency devaluation.[10] Such a devaluation results in an increase in the money income of the export sector and increased import prices.[11]

An alternative response to the problem of balance of payments was selective restrictions on imports; this option was taken throughout the "import substitution" period. However, this policy raised import prices and tended to bias private investment in the direction of the production of those products for which a home market existed but which were limited by import restrictions.[12] In particular, these restrictions resulted in the domestic production of the nonessentials previously imported, and led to increasing dependency on advanced capitalist countries for capital goods and on the domestic export sector to provide the foreign exchange necessary to finance these imports.

In this model, monopoly pricing serves as a mechanism for propagating price increases initiated in the agricultural and import sectors.[13] That is, monopoly or oligopoly in urban manufacture allows industry to pass on high cost-prices. This practice results in a wage-price inflationary spiral, as workers struggle against falling real wages. In addition, as industry contracts, government revenues (based largely on indirect taxes) fall, the central banking system is forced to extend credit.[14] It is important to understand what is meant by "forced." The ECLA school never denied that a tight money policy could prevent inflation. Their argument was, rather, that with autonomously rising food and import prices, slow growth in the money supply would result in lower prices elsewhere in the economy; more specifically, tight money would lower wages and industrial prices, reducing output and employment.[15] With respect to the proletariat, industrialization could only proceed if the wage share were to fall continuously. Therefore, a successful tight money program would require either very favorable external circumstances (a good market for exports to raise national income) or a repressive regime.

Monopoly also plays an important role in the explanation for the failure of import substitution. Import controls caused an influx of foreign manufacturing investment. In terms of the ECLA's model, such a development would appear to be very positive. Foreign investment would be a source of exchange, and should ease balance of payments pressures and reduce inflation. And, indeed, the ECLA's recommendations encouraged foreign investment during the mid-1950s.[16] However, industrial prices did not fall. This is alleged to have been due to monopoly/oligopoly pricing as well as to a lack of home markets brought about as a result of the continued reliance on exports.[17]

In any case, import substitution at the consumer level dwindled in the mid-1950s, and the collapse of the export market (following the end of the Korean War) dramatically increased Caribbean and Latin American balance of payments deficits, leading to currency devaluation and inflation. This, as well as the reformist character of the ECLA's later policy recommendations, led to a modification that was a part of an overall reorientation toward a theory of development emphasizing (1) the impossibility of autonomous capitalist development, and (2) underdevelopment as a normal result of capitalist development elsewhere in the world. The outcome of this theory of underdevelopment has been a reorganization, which varies from author to author, of the constituent parts of the ECLA's model (international division of labor, monopoly, and surplus transfer) in such a way as to produce the following result: given the influence of external forces, capitalist development is impossible; therefore, only socialist revolution will bring about economic growth in underdeveloped countries.

The theory of underdevelopment treats the capitalist mode of production as its object; that is, it argues that capitalist development proceeds by underdeveloping certain regions. Thus the theory is synchronic.[18] However, as it turns out, the various concepts employed in making this argument, and the consequent transmutation of Marx's concept of the capitalist mode of production, are the result of a recognition, represented ideologically, of the coexistence of different relations of production in a single social formation. As a consequence, concepts are employed *because* they do not belong to the concept of the capitalist mode of production; that is, by virtue of their ahistorical generality. Yet no attention is paid to the development of these "general concepts" because they are presented in terms of a redefinition of the capitalist mode of production.

With this context, I examine the "monopoly capital" version of the theory of underdevelopment (José Consuegra, Raul Fernandez), the theory of underdevelopment as a theory of surplus transfer (Arghiri Emmanuel, Paul Baran, Ruy Marini, André Gunder Frank), and the theory that underdevelopment is explained, fundamentally, by the international division of labor (Samir Amin and Clive Thomas).

The concept most prominently employed in an ahistorical manner in theories of development is that of monopoly. This concept also plays a role in structuralist economic theory, as we know, but it is in later theories that it dominates.

In Consuegra, for example, monopoly price is the sole cause of inflation in developing countries as well as in advanced capitalist countries.[19] Consuegra presents his argument in terms of an opposition between monopoly pricing and the quantity theory of money. According to him, Marx's remarks concerning the possibility of affecting prices through an increase in the quantity of symbolic money, rather than by the purely passive determination of the quantity of *commodity* money required to circulate, were overly influenced by the "metalist" theories prevalent at the time of Marx's writing. What is important in Marx's theory of money, according to Consuegra, is the one-way causality between the sum of prices and the quantity of money (symbolic or commodity) required to circulate.[20] Thus, following Marx, the state can never influence the price level through manipulations of the supply of money; it can only respond passively to changes in prices determined in production. As Consuegra puts the matter, "commodities enter the market with prices determined *by their* producers."[21] Their producers, in the age of monopoly capitalism, are monopolistic firms. Therefore, inflation is the expression of the capacity of monoplists to fix prices. This is easier in less developed countries, where capital is more concentrated, than in developed countries; consequently, the rate of inflation tends to be higher in developing countries than in the developed world.

The concept of monopoly is extended to cover all facets of the national and international economy; agricultural prices are inflated because of monopoly in agriculture (*concentration latifundista*), and import prices are high because of monopoly power in the center.[22] Moreover, prices are high for the same reason that capitalist development is impossible in Latin America and the Caribbean: capitalism is not competitive enough.

The notion that manipulation of the money supply cannot possibly affect prices is untenable. Monetary authorities may respond to prices that have increased for reasons unrelated to the supply of money by increasing this supply. If they do not, the effects on capitalist development may be disastrous, but it is not impossible for a tight money policy to lower the price level.

Furthermore, monopoly is treated in isolation from the process of centralization by which monopoly comes about, a process that temporarily reduces the number of firms in an industry. Without this recognition, there is no explanation for why capital does not flow into sectors that enjoy high monopoly profits. Moreover, to argue that stagnation of development is a necessary result of monopoly in developing countries is to ignore how a sector becomes monopolized in the first place: precisely, through the capitalist development of the forces of production.

Perhaps more importantly, divorcing monopoly pricing from centralization treats monopoly in an ahistorical way, i.e., as a supply restriction. A supply restriction can occur in any commodity-producing society, but monopoly based upon the centralization of the productive forces is peculiarly capitalist. What is unconsciously recognized in the use of such a concept to explain underdevelopment is that the dynamism generally associated with capitalism is absent. This absence is then explained by redefining capitalism as a nondynamic system, as one in which the driving force of capitalism (competition) has disappeared. As a result, social formations containing precapitalist relations are treated ideologically and not scientifically.

The second concept that derived from the ECLA model, and that has, in some cases, been expanded to explain the other aspects of this model, is that of surplus transfer. This concept is sometimes employed with monopoly (Baran) and sometimes rigorously separated from it (Emmanuel). The central idea here is that the transfer of surplus impedes by various mechanisms, the development of the periphery. For Baran, this transfer occurs through the repatriation of profits, made possible by foreign ownership of the means of production.[23] For most other writers, surplus is transferred via "unequal exchange." In this case, the transfer becomes evident in high import prices, balance of payment crises, devaluations, and inflation.

According to Marini, wages are suppressed in the periphery because periphery workers produce exports. Since the realization of the surplus value produced in the periphery is accomplished in the center, capital can force down wages in the periphery without encountering the limits imposed on capital in the center.[24] But, as Dore and Weeks point out, "under-consumption merely provides the mechanism by which the appropriation of surplus value by the center from the periphery occurs."[25] A somewhat similar approach is employed by Emmanuel.[26] Assuming prices and profits to be determined internationally and wages to be nationally determined, the price of exports for the low-wage country will be lower, and the price of imports higher, than they are where wages are equalized.

What is left unexplained in theories of surplus transfer is why, given low wages and the presence of capitalist relations in underdeveloped countries, capital does not flow into production there, raising wages, developing a home market, developing the forces of production and so on, until "unequal exchange" ceases to operate. That is to say, the transfer of surplus from one country to another does not prevent its transfer back again where the conditions of profitable production exist.[27]

In addition, while in some theories (especially that of Emmanuel), the term *surplus* is carefully defined, more often it is employed very loosely. In Frank, the terms *surplus*, *monopoly*, and *exploitation* are employed with reference to an identification between capitalism and commodity production.[28] Surplus is transferred through a "chain of metropolis/satellite relations," which characterize not only relations between center and periphery countries, but between regions of developing countries, between landlords and peasants, and between peasants and landless laborers. Again, a recognition of problems not amenable to treatment in a synchronic analysis is transformed into an attempt to solve these problems by categorically redefining the concepts proper to the capitalist mode of production.

Subsequent theories of development have not improved upon the work of the structuralist theories of the 1950s. They have merely reorganized the causal elements and appended certain political conclusions. The core of the argument remains the same: the international division of labor, at the time of the Caribbean and Latin America's integration into the world market, forced peripheral countries to specialize in agricultural goods and raw materials, and this fact underdeveloped peripheral agriculture and industry in such a way that the pattern of specialization tends to be reproduced in the transfer of surplus out of the periphery—guaranteeing continued underdevelopment.

In fact, the writer who has most exhaustively synthesized the various parts of the theory of underdevelopment, Samir Amin, has essentially rewritten the ECLA argument in terms of several new theoretical devices.[29] The international division of labor, through a trade mechanism ruled by absolute cost advantage, guarantees the maintenance of precapitalist elements in the periphery. This lowers wages by providing cheap labor power. Low wages mean unequal exchange, high import prices, balance of payment crises; in short, the pattern of specialization is reproduced, as is the argument of Raul Prebisch.

This modification, however, does not make the argument any stronger; it still fails to explain why capital does not move into low-wage areas, importing techniques and producing nonagricultural goods for export and for domestic consumption. However, it is rather interesting that Amin ties surplus transfer to the concept of absolute cost advantage. Prebisch's initial critique was of the comparative advantage trade theory, by which both trading partners benefit from specialization, even in those cases in which one partner can produce all commodities more efficiently. He argued that trade will transfer surplus to the more advanced country because of its absolute advantage, which takes the form of specializing in the more desirable export (manufacture). All of the theories of surplus transfer have repeated this procedure: supplanting the theory of comparative cost advantage with one based on absolute cost advantage, and then detailing the form of surplus transfer that takes place.

All of these modifications of the critique of comparative advantage have missed the central point: the theory relies upon the assumption that capitalist relations dominate both countries. Where this assumption is untrue, the argument does not work. If the agricultural producing country does not increase production in its area of specialty, then both countries suffer. This is only to say, of course, that the development of the capitalist mode of production, whether it is defined within a nation-state or at the level of the world economy, is limited and conditioned by the existence of precapitalist production relations.

The central problem raised by the development of underdevelopment school is described by Foster-Carter[30] as that of deciding upon the units of analysis. That is, should the relations of production of an activity in an LDC be described according to the class relations it involves, or by virture of its relationship to the capitalist world economy? More broadly, is the cause of the maintenance of precapitalist relations of production to be found in the needs of the capitalist world system, or is the existence of noncapitalist relations of production a cause of underdevelopment?

It is fair to say that writers who have chosen to defend the capitalist world system point of view have been unable to describe the role of several of Marx's more important concepts, such as class and exploitation, without altering these concepts dramatically. However, this in itself does not diminish the significance of the question of the relative importance of internal class relations vis-à-vis external relations with the world economy. A vitally important task for development theory is to develop a class analysis of production relations on an international level. We will discuss this issue in more detail in later chapters. In the following section, I will briefly review a recent debate on agrarian transformation, which bears upon our subsequent analysis and, as we shall see, turns on the same "units of analysis" question.

THE AGRARIAN QUESTION

The debate concerning the cause of underdevelopment at the international level has an interesting parallel in discussions of agrarian transformation at national and regional levels. The traditional Marxist view that capitalism will inevitably act as a catalyst for progressive change in the forces of production appears to fly in the face of several facts of life in less developed countries, particularly with respect to the stubborn persistence of underdevelopment in agriculture. Debates over the interpretation of this phenomenon focus once again on the question of the ultimate cause of underdevelopment.

Marx's own theory concerning the transition to capitalism is discussed in greater detail below, but it has been interpreted as predicting the dissolution of precapitalist relations and the destruction of the classes associated with them. In the classic English case, peasants were expropriated by landlords, and subsequently proletarianized. Landlords themselves engaged in a protracted class struggle, ultimately to be defeated by industrial capitalists. While the specific details would vary widely from country to country, the ultimate "victory" of capital rested on its ability to develop the forces of production. Given the more or less complete commoditization of production, ceaseless revolutions in technology guaranteed the destruction of any classes that might compete with the capitalist class.

In *The Development of Capitalism in Russia*, Lenin described alternative paths of transition.[31] The feudal estate could be capitalized by the landlord, some former tenants hired as wage laborers and others expelled as surplus population ("Junker" road). Alternatively, the landlord might only capitalize a portion of the estate, so that some peasants obtain title to their land. However, the existence of an independent peasantry is an inherently transitory phenomenon. The difference is only that the segmentation of the peasantry takes place outside of the (now capitalist) estate. Some peasants join the rural bourgeoisie; the vast majority ultimately join the landless proletariat. I do not mean to trivialize the distinction. On the contrary, it is quite important; as Lenin argues, the Kulak class becomes key to the development of the home market. The point I want to emphasize is simply that in the classic Marxist texts the destruction of precapitalist relations was considered inevitable.

This classical progressivist point of view runs counter to the stylized facts of underdevelopment. In Latin America and the Caribbean, as in much of the Third World today, the transition to capitalism in agriculture, by which I mean the complete transformation of the rural population into sellers and buyers of labor power, and the organization of production on this basis, is blocked.

Not only is the transformation incomplete, but in many cases precapitalist relations seem to persist. In particular, peasant agriculture (nonspecialized use-value production) provides cheap labor power to commercial agriculture. Semiproletarian rural workers can be hired at wages below subsistence, because these workers/peasants produce a portion of their own subsistence at whatever rate of "self-exploitation" is required.[32] This phenomena has been dubbed *functional dualism*.[33] As a consequence, increased commoditization of agriculture has not resulted in the transformation of production relations.

The interpretation of these facts leads back to the units of analysis debate with which we ended the previous section. For the development of underdevelopment school, these precapitalist relations are merely the form through which surplus is expropriated from direct producers, ultimately to be transferred to the center. That is, the class relations at the point of production are less important than the fact that capitalism is the dominant force at the world level. Ernesto Laclau has attacked this "trade-centered" viewpoint, insisting upon a class analysis of production in Latin American agriculture.[34] He concludes that "semi-feudal conditions are still widely characteristic of the Latin American countryside."[35] A related rejection of the world system approach is contained in the work of the "articulation of modes of production" school. I will discuss this approach in detail in later chapters. Roughly speaking, however, their argument is that underdevelopment consists of capitalist relations of production being blocked as a result of the relations established among modes of production within a social formation. This viewpoint is most fully explored by Pierre-Phillipe Rey.[36]

The most consistent extension of the Frank-Wallerstein approach into the discussion of agrarian transformation is the "concealed wage" argument of Banaji.[37] Banaji argues that peasant production, under the domination of capitalism, is only formally precapitalist. In reality, peasant simple commodity production is already a capitalist relation of production. The price paid to a peasant producer is a concealed wage.[38] To the extent that peasants produce subsistence use-values, they contribute to the reduction of the value of labor power, so that once again, the relations of production are capitalist. And, once again, the (internal) class relations are viewed as largely irrelevant; what is important is the nexus (thru exchange) that formally precapitalist relations shares with capitalism at the world level.

The problem with this approach is that it glosses over any implications that the maintenance of precapitalist relations might have for accumulation and class struggle. The form of class struggle, the role of the state, and the nature of accumulation will all be affected by the fact that the peasantry retains the means of production. Capitalist control over the production process is limited in a fundamental sense and must be accomplished by means other than the extension of relative surplus value production, i.e., through the action of the state and other means. In addition, the resistance to capitalist control will not be likely to take classical proletarian forms.

CONCLUSION

I have examined, in this chapter, the development of underdevelopment school, and the extension of its ideas into the agrarian question. Critics of the Frank-Wallerstein approach have argued that it ignores the relations of production. It creates problems as well, in the analysis of the rural economy, where followers of Frank and Wallerstein have tended to ignore the class questions associated with the maintenance of precapitalist relations.

Nevertheless, while it is true that an adequate analysis of accumulation and distribution in the context of development requires a class analysis at the point of production, it is equally true that any understanding of the phenomenon of underdevelopment must be informed by a class analysis at the international level. If not, the Third World will not be represented theoretically in any specific way. It is with this goal in mind—to produce an analysis of economic calculation and accumulation appropriate to less developed countries, which does not merely transplant the facts of European economic development—that we turn to a more rigorous analysis of the concept of economic transition. We begin with a review of the philosophical underpinnings of the "articulation of modes of production" school.

NOTES

1. Etienne Balibar, "On the Basic Concepts of Historical Materialism," in Louis Althusser and Etienne Balibar, *Reading Capital*, trans. Ben Brewster (London: New Left Books, 1977), p. 301.

2. André Gunder Frank, *Latin America: Underdevelopment or Revolution?* (New York: Monthly Review Press, 1969).

3. Immanuel Wallerstein, *The Modern World-System: Capitalist Agriculture and the Origins of the European World Economy in the Sixteenth Century* (New York: Academic Press, 1974).

4. Among writers on the Caribbean, this perspective is represented by W. Rodney, *How Europe Underdeveloped Africa* (Dar es Salaam and London: Tanzania Publishing House and Bogle L'Ouverture Publications, 1972); E. Williams, *Capitalism and Slavery* (London: André Deutsch, 1964); C. Thomas, *Dependence and Transformation: The Economics of the Transition to Socialism* (New York and London: Monthly Review Press, 1974).

5. Not to be confused with the structuralism of Althusser and his followers.

6. Raul Fernandez, "Imperialist Capitalism in the Third World: Theory and Evidence from Colombia," *Latin American Perspectives*, No. 79 (Winter, 1979), p. 40; also see Anthony Brewer, *Marxist Theories of Imperialism, A Critical Survey* (London: Routledge & Kegan Paul, 1980), pp. 177–79.

7. Celso Furtado, *Economic Development of Latin America*, second edition (Cambridge: Cambridge University Press, 1976), p. 121.

8. David Felix, "An Alternative View of the 'Monetarist'–'Structuralist' Controversy," *Latin American Issues, Essays and Comments*, ed. Albert O. Hirschman (New York: The Twentieth Century Fund, 1961), p. 88.

9. ECLA, *Development Problems in Latin America* (Austin: University of Texas Press, 1969), p. xv.

10. R. Bernal, "Resolving the Debt Crisis," U.W.I. Monograph #1, 1985, Kingston, Jamaica; also see N. Girvan, "Notes on Jamaica's External Debt," U.W.I. Monograph, 1985, Kingston, Jamaica.

11. Furtado, p. 118.

12. Felix, p. 89.

13. Osvaldo Sunkel, "Un esquema general para el analisis de la inflacion," *Economia*, No. 62 (1959), p. 86.

14. Felix, p. 84.

15. *Ibid*.

16. ECLA, pp. xxxiii–xxxiv.

17. Felix, p. 90.

18. Precapitalist relations are sometimes brought into the argument, but the maintenance of such structures is always considered to be a result (never a cause) of the underdevelopment of capitalism in the social formation. For examples, see Paul Baran, *The Political Economy of Growth* (New York: Monthly Review Press, 1968); and Samir Amin, *Accumulation on a World Scale* (New York: Monthly Review Press, 1974).

19. Jose Consequegra, *Un nuevo enfogue de la teoria de la inflacion* (Bogota: Ediciones Tercer Mundo, 1976), p. 122.

20. *Ibid*, pp. 83–94.

21. *Ibid*, p. 111, emphasis mine, MKP.

22. *Ibid*, pp. 122–124.

23. Baran, pp. 134–163.

24. Ruy Marini, *La dialectica de la dependencia* (Mexico City: Ediciones Era, 1975).

25. Elizabeth Dore and John Weeks, "International Exchange and the Causes of Backwardness" (Washington, D.C., 1979, unpublished paper), p. 32.

26. Emmanuel, *Unequal Exchange*.

27. Brewer, pp. 226–30.

28. Frank, pp. 236–40.

29. Amin.

30. A. Foster-Carter, "The Modes of Production Controversy," *New Left Review*, No. 107 (Jan.–Feb. 1978).

31. V. I. Lenin, *The Development of Capitalism in Russia* (Moscow: Progress Publishers, 1964).

32. David Goodman and Michael Redclift, *From Peasant to Proletarian: Capitalist Development and Agrarian Transitions* (New York: St. Martin's Press, 1982), p. 78.

33. Alain de Janvry, *The Agrarian Question and Reformism in Latin America* (Baltimore: Johns Hopkins, 1981), p. 39.

34. Ernesto Laclau, "Feudalism and Capitalism in Latin America," *New Left Review*, No. 67 (1971).

35. Laclau, p. 31.

36. Pierre-Phillipe Rey, *Les Alliances des Classes* (Paris: Maspero, 1973).

37. J. Banaji, "Modes of Production in a Materialist Conception of History," *Capital and Class*, vol. 3 (Autumn, 1977).

38. Banaji, p. 34.

3

INTRODUCTION TO STRUCTURALISM

The issues associated with the transition to capitalism have been discussed mostly within two separate strands of thought. These are distinguished by their different outlook on epistemology, the nature of Marxist science, and on political issues. They have also been developed for the most part on opposite sides of the English Channel. The work of English historians on the transition to capitalism represents possibly the finest application in postwar intellectual history of Marxist theory to a concrete problem.[1] However, the French Structuralists, followers of Louis Althusser, are more theoretically introspective. This level of self-awareness makes the French school more immediately relevant to the current undertaking, because I wish to extend the principles developed in the study of transition to capitalism in Europe to those contemporary problems grouped together under the title of "theory of economic development." Consequently, I will postpone, for the most part, discussion of the British historians' work on the transition until after the procedures for studying the transition suggested by Althusser, Balibar, and others have been examined in the abstract.[2]

The following remarks are designed to introduce Structuralism. I will discuss some of the tenants of Althusser's thinking, as well as the main criticisms that have been brought to bear against them. I will also examine those collaborators and/or followers of Althusser whose work bears directly on the analysis of the transition (Balibar, Bettelheim, and Rey). Then I will outline the methodology to be utilized in the present work, a methodology that draws heavily upon the work of the writers discussed in this section.

In presenting Althusser, I will first describe the discourse within which his work appeared. This discourse was a product of a conjuncture of political events within the world Communist movement—specifically, the Twentieth Congress of the Communist Party of the Soviet Union (1956) and the dawning of Sino-Soviet contention. The terms of the debates surrounding these events were set by a long-standing question in twentieth-century Marxism: is Marxism a science? In focussing on the development of Structuralist thought in this context, I will ignore (1) the important influences upon this movement by non-Marxist Structuralists (Levi-Strauss, Foucault, Lacan, Saussure, and many others), and (2) the relation of Althusser's thought to bourgeois social theory in general.[3] An appreciation of the political conjuncture at the time of Althusser's writing sheds light on the epistemological issues discussed below: the critique of empiricism (and its relation to humanism), the analysis of Marx's break, the concept of structure, and structural causality.

ALTHUSSER AND HIS FOLLOWERS

In the early 1960s, when Althusser began publishing his major essays, the predominant influence upon Marxist debates was the growing split in the international workers' movement occasioned by the dispute between the Soviet Union and the People's Republic of China.[4] One effect of this split was to consolidate the revisionist Communist parties (the Communist Party of the Soviet Union, and its subsidiary communist parties in Europe and elsewhere) around (1) defense of the Soviet Union through its peaceful coexistence with the United States, (2) parliamentary reforms in capitalist countries, and (3) alliance with the progressive bourgeoisie in less developed countries. Against this development arose the Chinese Communist Party's challenge. In those years, the Chinese line appeared to offer a return to Marxism-Leninism in theory backed up by an alternative revolutionary experience. Interestingly, it was in the rhetoric of de-Stalinization and in the name of socialist humanism that the revisionist Communist parties chose to defend themselves.[5] Although Althusser was writing from within the French Communist Party, he was critical of the domination of the Communist movement by Khrushchev and had been heavily influenced by the Chinese Communist Party line.[6] Thus, he attacked humanism for being a *right* deviation. Althusser's attack was directed both against the humanist revival of Marx's early works, a revival with roots outside of the Soviet Union that predated the Twentieth Congress, as well as against Soviet socialist humanism.[7]

However, Althusser rapidly carried his critique of humanism beyond the arena of international politics into that of Marxist epistemology, which has been dominated in this century by a conflict between the Second International and the historicist movement (stemming from the work of

Georg Lukacs).[8] The issue of chief concern to Althusser was the scientific basis of political economy.

The Political Economy of the Second International was based upon Engel's book *Dialectics of Nature*, in which Hegel's dialectic is reconceptualized as a natural law.[9] Social change, as an object of knowledge, is reduced to a reflection of changes in the economic base of society that would inevitably lead to socialism. As Lucio Colletti has said, however, such a reduction of reality to the reflection of the movement of a single idea, even where that idea is the idea of matter (natural law), is a thinly veiled form of the (absolute) idealism of Hegel.[10]

For historicism,[11] a theory only comprehends the world in so far as it grasps it as a totality. But this comprehension requires an identity of subject and object, since "thought can only grasp what it has itself created."[12] This identity, however, is precisely what is lost in commodity fetishism, in which discrete things are bound together, not by any consciousness whatsoever, but by the market.[13] Only in the proletariat, in whose consciousness (as a class), the commodity (as labor power) is rendered self-conscious, are subject and object identified. Therefore, only under the dictatorship of the proletariat are the limits placed upon knowledge by capitalism surpassed.

For Althusser, if neither of these epistemologies can found a science of political economy, it is because they share a common error: the identification of objects of thought with real objects. He refers to this misconception sometimes as empiricism and, in other places, as humanism. However, the two concepts are related in this respect. Empiricism, for Althusser, refers to the view that knowledge consists of a grasping of the essence of an object by a subject.[14] But the possibility of such a grasping implies that the subject and object are already connected, although perhaps in a precognitive way. Knowledge is a drawing out of something that is already present in the subject-object relation. Consequently, empiricism is the epistemological form of humanism: the subject is the center of the universe.

Most importantly, humanism is the basis for modern ideology,[15] and in particular for the attempts to base political economy on the ideology examined above. We have seen that the dialectic of nature employed by Second International Marxism was a version of Hegel's dialectic, where the latter is a term for a relation between the subject and the object in which the object is ultimately reduced to an aspect of the subject, that is, to a reflection of it (spirit). In the adaptation of Hegel's work from the *Dialectics of Nature* and *Anti-Duhring*,[16] which nourished the Second International, nature replaced spirit, but the observable world remained a reflection. Furthermore, the connection of subject and object was translated into a relation of reflection between an economic base and a (political and ideological) superstructure, which prohibited any autonomy in the development of the superstructure. In any case, the assimilation of empirical reality to an aspect of an *idea* (that is, the complicity of subject and object) prohibits a scientific, as opposed to an ideological, foundation for political economy.[17] The difference between science and ideology, for Althusser, is that while ideology can only offer a closed system, science is open to internal development; that is, ideology is limited to ratifying or rejecting propositions imposed upon it from the outside.[18] An example would be, presumably, the use to which automatic Marxism was put by the Second International: because socialism in advanced countries was inevitable, the interim role of working-class parties was limited to the mitigation of the *effects* of capitalism.

For Althusser, the thought object is not identified with any object in reality. That is to say, reality is not immediately present in the phenomena accessible to observations; rather, the pursuit of scientific knowledge acts upon raw materials that are already "thought objects," not independent facts. Therefore, the basis of knowledge is not a complicity of subject and object, as for historicism, and the attempts to found political economy on such a complicity can only produce ideology—whether it be proletarian or bourgeois ideology—not knowledge.

Considered in the context of the political and philosophical conjunctures in which Althusser wrote "On the Young Marx,"[19] his argument that Marx broke with his own previous work in the writing of *The German Ideology*[20] takes on special significance. For the break was with humanism and with ideology, in favor of science; that is to say, the break was with the very same ideology which had been placed on the agenda by de-Stalinization and the Sino-Soviet split. Prior to 1845, Marx had analyzed civil society, i.e., commodity producing society, using concepts which, although specifically informed by the humanism of Ludwig Feuerbach, were similar to those employed by the early Adam Smith and, later, by Jeremy Bentham. Civil society was characterized by alienated human essence, by human essence in a distorted form, in a word, by *competition* between individuals. Of course, for Marx, unlike other humanists, communism was required to realign society and human nature. However, the essential epistemological *prise de position* was the same: the truth (or essence) of civil society was present in its appearance. By replacing the concept of human nature with that of social relations, argues Althusser, Marx broke decisively with the humanist/empiricist basis of his early work and established Marxism's scientific foundation.

According to Althusser, this foundation, as Marx developed it throughout the remainder of his life, consists in the construction of certain concepts, especially those of the relations and forces of production. The former refers to the social division of labor and the latter to the labor process considered more or less technically. The particular combination of relations and forces of production defines a mode of production; however, a mode of production is not purely economic. Nor is it characterized by noneconomic aspects which reflect economic ones. Rather, the concept of society as base and superstructure is replaced, by Althusser, with one which sees society as a structure with relatively autonomous levels: economic, political and ideological.

Althusser makes two important points about this structure. First, the structure of society is not visible in its operation. History is opaque. This is a much different use of Marx's concept of fetishism than that employed by historicists, for whom fetishism describes capitalist reality. For Althusser, the concept is generalized to a necessary dislocation between the way society operates and the way in which its operations appear. This applies to all modes of production, not just to capitalism. Secondly, each level exists in its own time and develops according to a rhythm that is not determined by the other levels. For example, the development of political structure is not determined as a manisfestation or reflection of the economic base. Consequently, a mode of production does not develop in unified (historical) time. It is never possible to locate all the elements of a mode of production in a single moment, at a particular time.[21] Thus, the unity of a mode of production is not historical, for it does not result from the coexistence of various levels in historical time, but from the special type of dominance exercised by the economic level over the other levels of a mode of production. According to Althusser's notion of structure in dominance, the specific contradiction between the relations and forces of production in a mode of production determines which of the instances (economic, political, ideological) is to be the dominant instance, that is, which is to provide the unity of the structure. Lower levels of abstraction are referred to as social formations. While there exists some confusion over this term, especially in Balibar's treatment, I argue below that it is best conceived as an interlacing of several modes of production.

Althusser employs the term "conjuncture" to establish a level of discussion in which the effects of the relatively autonomous levels of activity are reunited with historical time, showing how their uneven development, vis-à-vis each other, creates special conditions. His example is Lenin's analysis of Russia in 1917, in which he showed it to be the weakest link in the chain of imperialism.[22] This leads us to the concept of structural causality. Althusser rejects both linear causality and expressive causality. By the former, Althusser refers to causal relations between events. In academic philosophy, this is called material cause (after Aristotle's distinction), and it is, of course, the notion of cause that predominates in contemporary philosophy. By referring to it as linear, Althusser highlights the fact that causal relations between events are dependent upon the very time frame that Althusser has rejected as empiricist:

a unified, historical time in which society (as a whole) develops. By rejecting expressive causality, Althusser rejects Hegel's theory of reflection,[23] in which causality is reduced to a relation of meaning (the meaning of the whole exists in each of its parts). According to Althusser, causality is structural. Because Althusser's treatment of structural causality is often cryptic and enigmatic,[24] some explanation of this important concept, which has received considerable criticism, might prove helpful.

Althusser develops his concept of causality as a critique of the distinction between essence and phenomenon dominating empiricist epistemology.[25] This distinction is present in both of the causal theories discussed above. In the case of linear causality, the essence lies beneath the phenomenon as a (causal) pattern to be discovered by generalization from observation. For expressive causality, the phenomena are illusions or reflections of essence. In either view, essence and phenomena are opposed and yet connected in some fundamental manner. Althusser replaces the concept of essence with that of structured relations among appearances. The structure of society, which only exists as a relation between the elements of society, is the cause, yet this cause does not lie beneath appearances, nor is it external to the operation of society in any way. Cause is nothing besides the effect of a structure on its elements. Consequently, the construction of scientific concepts adequate to an understanding of the relations between elements of society is, at the same time, the procedure for understanding the structure of society.

Some responses to Althusser have been made primarily on political grounds. E. P. Thompson's description of Althusser's work as "Stalinism reduced to the paradigm of theory,"[26] falls into this category. More theoretical critiques divide into two groups: those that essentially counterpose empiricist views to different anti-empiricist propositions of Althusser, and those that attempt to take Althusser on his own ground, arguing that he has failed in his attempt to put Marxism on a scientific footing (here we find the critiques of Alex Callinicos and André Glucksmann).

If we recall Althusser's claim that the raw material of scientific enquiry is already theory (and not fact) by virtue of having been constituted as an "object of knowledge,"[27] it is not altogether surprising that he should be accused of idealism by those who place emphasis on the theory-neutrality of facts. This is one of the criticisms that Thompson levels at Althusser in the *Poverty of Theory*.[28] The argument is that no new knowledge can be produced from the action of cognition if theories, in effect, produce their own facts; moreover, no dialogue can take place between concepts and "the phenomena of material and social existence."[29] The presumption, of course, is that new knowledge is found by appeal to something external to theory.

Now, it is obvious, first of all, that this formulation begs the question of how knowledge is produced (or obtained). Secondly, this argument displays a certain naiveté in that, in this respect, Althusser's proposition is neither new nor even radically anti-empiricist. Kant made fundamentally the same point when he distinguished between unknowable things-in-themselves and sense data that were accessible to science because they were already conceived in terms of certain basic neutral categories. This critique of theory-neutral facts has been echoed throughout the philosophy of science,[30] and has even trickled down into such philosophical provinces as bourgeois economics.[31] In any case, simply expressing the view that knowledge consists in an appropriation of external reality by the subject, thereby counterposing empiricism to Althusser, fails to prove very much.

The same holds true for the more sophisticated critique of Althusser by Hindess and Hirst.[32] To these writers, the weak link in Althusser's system is his concept of structural causality. Their reason is that this concept denies the existence of any external cause, the capitalist mode of production, for example, causes its *own* reproduction. For Hindess and Hirst, this way of looking at things is idealist, and they seek to replace it with the essentially descriptive concept of "mode of production." That is, whenever, as a result of class struggle, conditions conducive to the existence of a mode of production occur, that mode will exist, but a mode of production cannot *cause* its own conditions of existence. Causal relations are linear relations between events; concepts like "relations of production" and "forces of production" are descriptive. This critique plays an important role in Hindess' and Hirst's analysis of transition, and thus I will examine it principally later and in that context. For the moment, simply note that Hindess and Hirst have counterposed an empiricist notion (in this case, an idea of causality that has already been dealt with extensively by Althusser) to the concept employed by Althusser.

Other writers have taken Althusser more seriously, but find that his project, when examined on its own grounds, ultimately fails. The problem for Callinicos and Glucksmann,[33] is that Althusser never answers, in a completely satisfactory manner, the question of how, if theoretical practice is autonomous, the development of concepts in such a practice is related to other social practices (economic, political, and ideological)? Without an answer to this question, science is left up in the air, outside of and beyond any capacity to transform the world. Any successful attempt to understand Marxism as such a science would seem dubious in the extreme.[34]

The answer to this question suggested by Althusser in *For Marx* is clearly inadequate.[35] There, he claims that theoretical practice is related to other practices by virtue of a *structure* common to all practices. This, however, is but a slightly modified empiricist argument: thought can appropriate reality because thought and reality have the same structure.[36] That is, epistemology is here based upon a preexisting complicity between subject and object; Althusser's solution is empiricist by his own definition.

In later works, however, and particularly in *Lenin and Philosophy and Other Essays*,[37] Althusser approaches the problem in a different way, that is, Marx was able to break with ideology because he had taken a proletarian position in philosophy. Callinicos feels that this alteration rescues Althusser's system.[38] However, it could be argued that identifying Marx's break with a proletarian class position involves a return to the version of historicism for which a theory is scientific in so far as it serves the need of a particular class. For example, what are we to make of the application of his general concept of dissimulation to postcapitalist society? Does ideology exist in the Communist mode of production or is Communist society transparent to its members? Of more immediate importance is the question, if workers live, necessarily, under ideology, then how can proletarian class consciousness be possible?

Serious questions remain unanswered by Althusser's system. However, I am in strong accord with the general purpose of Althusser's intervention: to establish Marxism on a scientific footing, in such a way that concrete problems can be solved in a scientific (nonideological) manner. Furthermore, I agree with the identification of ideology with empiricism/humanism. Consequently, in this study of attempts to analyze the transition to capitalism, I will adopt Althusser's interpretation of Marxism, broadly defined and qualified in several respects (see below), as a standard against which these attempts can be measured.

I turn now to some brief remarks on other Marxist structuralists who have contributed to the study of transitions from one mode of production to another. I will discuss Balibar's extension of Althusser's work in the direction of a general theory of modes of production (including Hindess' and Hirst's criticism of such an approach), Charles Bettelheim's important contribution to the study of transitions, and Pierre-Phillippe Rey's treatment of the transition as an articulation of the capitalist mode of production with other modes of production.

Balibar[39] sets out to develop a general theory of modes of production. He argues that any mode of production can be analyzed as a specific combination of the same basic elements: laborer, means of production, and nonlaborer.[40] Those elements are connected in two different ways: (1) by a property connection (a social division of labor) and (2) by a real appropriation connection (a reference to the labor process or the technical division of labor). These connections are new names for the relations and forces of production, respectively. The connections may be in correspondence with each other, as in the capitalist mode of production, or they may not correspond to each other, as in the period of manufacture, which Balibar calls a transitional mode of production. Where the relations and forces are in correspondence, the effect of the relations on the forces is to develop those forces in a manner that reproduces the mode of production. In capitalism, the forces of production develop in such a way as to place the labor process under the control of capital. Where the connections are not in correspondence, the effect of the relations of production is to transform the forces of production, previously developed in such a way as to reproduce an earlier mode of production, into a form of development that reproduces the new mode of production. In the transitional mode of production, capitalist relations of production transform a handicraft labor process into a capitalist process through mechanization of the labor process. Balibar also examines other forms of noncorrespondence characterizing transitional modes of production. These I discuss in later sections.

As we have seen above, Hindess and Hirst have criticized structural causality, seeking to replace it with a linear causality between events (or "class struggle") in real history. For them, Marx's concepts, such as mode of production, are theoretical instruments designed to explain causal relations between events. This critique is closely related to their rejection of any general theory of modes of production. They argue, first of all, that structural causality prohibits the possibility of any transition from one mode of production to another, precisely because structural causality implies an eternal reproduction of structure. If a mode of production produces its own conditions of existence, how can a transition to another mode occur? Therefore, they point out that, using such a theory, one cannot adequately distinguish a transitional mode of production from a nontransitional one. And here Hindess' and Hirst's critique is valuable, for it highlights the central difficulty encountered in treating transition on the same level of abstraction as modes of production. I will in fact argue against such a procedure in Chapter 3.

However, Hindess and Hirst contend, further, that Balibar's difficulties in defining the transition stem from the fact that structural causality is really only expressive causality, that is, that the concept of structure is really no different from essence and the effects of the structure on its elements is really nothing but the outer manifestation of inner essence. Furthermore, they argue, since a general theory of modes of production requires that each mode be seen as a variant form of a single general structure (the elements of a mode of production and the connections between them), such a general theory amounts to nothing more than an expression of a general structure (essence) in the real phenomena of history.[41] In a later work, *Mode of Production and Social Formation*, this line of reasoning leads Hindess and Hirst to reject entirely the notion of mode of production.[42]

I do not agree that Althusser's and Balibar's position can so easily be reduced to an Hegelian philosophy of history. First of all, a structural relation between elements of a mode of production is not the same as an essence, the qualities of which are expressed in outer phenomena. Secondly, Hindess and Hirst seem to have imposed upon Althusser the very empiricist opposition between theory and reality that Althusser has rejected. For Hindess and Hirst, a mode of production (theory) is opposed to its conditions of existence (which occur in real history). For them, this opposition is resolved in the discovery of causal patterns (by the application of theory to reality). Hindess and Hirst accuse Althusser of employing a concept of causality (structural) in which a mode of production guarantees its own conditions of existence, as if structural causality were a relation between theory and reality.

If the above remarks are correct, then Hindess and Hirst have severely misinterpreted Althusser's use of levels of abstraction. The relation between two levels of analysis, say between mode of production and social formation or conjuncture, is neither a relation between the object of thought and real object, nor a series of better and better approximations to the real object.[43] Rather, the relation between levels of abstraction involves a systematic reconsideration of issues on the basis of the introduction of more complex elements into the analysis. For example, we have the social formation, in which elements of the various modes of production interact, and the conjuncture, exhibiting a degree of complexity in which various levels (economic, political, ideological) develop unevenly and coincide at a particular moment. Most importantly, if causal relations differ at various levels of abstraction, it is not because causality is less or more structural or less or more internal at one level of abstraction than at another, but because the structure is a different one. This should be clear from Althusser's analysis of Lenin's weakest link argument.[44] In this argument, the specific conjuncture of relatively autonomously developing instances, the coexistence of feudal agrarian structure, an immense and bureaucratic state apparatus, a weak bourgeoisie, and the demands of an imperialist war create the condition for a revolutionary rupture. Aspects of reality that would be impossible to bring together at other levels of analysis are here related, and their relationship is internal to the structure at hand.

Thus, while I cannot agree with Hindess' and Hirst's reduction of structuralism to a philosophy of history, implicit in Hindess' and Hirst's work is useful critique of the treatment of transition as a mode of production. In constructing a concept of transitional social formation (see Chapter 3), I will follow the method implied by Charles Bettelheim in *Economic Calculation and Forms of Property*.[45]

Bettelheim extends the concepts found in *Reading Capital* to an analysis of the transition to socialism. Of particular importance are Althusser's general concept of dissimulation (the opacity of history) and Balibar's idea of noncorrespondence as characteristic of transitions. The first leads Bettelheim to place special emphasis on the form taken by social labor in different modes of production and the expression of this form in economic calculation. In capitalism, for example, social labor takes the form of relations between commodities, of value, but this is not the case in other modes of production. Consequently, the presence of commodity categories in a social formation in transition to socialism indicates the existence of elements of the capitalist mode of production in that social formation.

The noncorrespondence that pertains to the transition to socialism is that between capitalist relations of production, which are indicated by the presence of commodity relations and are rooted in the operation of partially independent state enterprises, and the socialist legal form (state ownership) in which those capitalist relations appear. The expansion of capitalist relations in this form has certain effects upon the operation of the social formation Bettelheim sets out to analyze. It is important to note that Bettelheim analyzes transition as a special type of social formation, in which elements of various modes of production coexist, but in which no mode of production is dominant. I will employ this concept of transitional social formation in analyzing the transition to capitalism and development theory.

Finally, I will mention one last Structuralist, Pierre-Phillippe Rey, whose work will bear on later chapters.[46] Rey treats the transition to capitalism as an articulation of the capitalist mode of production with other, precapitalist, modes. Against certain writers who have argued that capitalism underdevelops some regions of the globe, Rey maintains that capitalism seeks everywhere to breakdown precapitalist relations of production and establish itself as the dominant mode. The success of the capitalist mode, in this respect, depends upon the effectiveness with which the precapitalist mode resists capitalism. Certain modes of production are extremely resistant, such as the lineage mode of production, existing in Africa prior to and during the colonial period. Others, such as feudalism, actually aid the development of capitalism. Despite many limitations, which will be discussed below, Rey's work signifies a pioneer effort in that he presents the transition in terms of the coexistence of, and struggle between, elements of various modes of production or, more precisely, in terms of a struggle between the classes defined by various modes of production.

While generally following Althusser and Balibar in their attempt to establish a scientific basis for Marxism and for the analysis of underdevelopment, I part company with Balibar over the issue of a transitional mode of production and will argue for the superiority of Bettelheim's transitional social formation. It is also necessary for me to clarify my position on two other subjects: last-instance economic determination, and the base-superstructure metaphor. On the matter of economic determination, Marx wrote:

the economic structure is the real basis on which the juridical and political superstructure is raised, and to which definite forms of thought correspond . . . all this is very true for our own times, in which material interests preponderate, but not for the Middle Ages, in which Catholicism, nor for Athens and Rome, where politics, reigned supreme. . . . This much, however, is clear, that the Middle Ages could not live on Catholicism, nor the ancient world on politics. On the contrary, it is the mode in which they gained livelihood that explains why here politics, and there Catholicism, played the chief part.[47]

In answer to bourgeois critics of Marx who have argued that the fact that the ancient world was not dominated by the economic sphere proves Marx wrong, Althusser and Balibar have interpreted the above passage to mean that the infrastructure (conceived as a combination of productive forces and relations of production) determines (that is, selects as if from a list of candidates) which level dominates a society. In this sense, the economic instance (over) determines events at other levels. However, last-instance determination is a clumsy formulation of Marx's procedure. Recall that the relations of production refer to a system of functions assigned to agents in respect to the way in which they interact with the means of production. Now it is clear from a large variety of historical and anthropological studies that these functions can be performed under the aegis of a variety of institutions. Kinship, religion, politics, and economics can constitute, separately or in combination, the relations of production. And, in so far as they do, they play the dominant role in social reproduction. But this says nothing about the institutional nature of the relations that function as production relations.[48]

What Marx does in the remarks quoted above is to theorize the universal existence of a hierarchy among the functions, which must be assumed by social relations if a society is to exist as such and reproduce itself.[49] In this sense, the "economic," defined broadly as material production, is always determinant, but there is little point in confusing this broad sense of the word with a narrower sense for which "economic" refers to the operation of the law of value, for the law of value is only determinant in the capitalist mode of production.

Several of Marx's most important concepts, notably the concepts of dissimulation and of economic determination, are often crammed into an architectural metaphor, using the terms *base* and *superstructure*, which does not do them justice. Here society is likened to a building, with an economic infrastructure that not only holds the building up but also causes it to have certain superstructural (political and ideological) features. Althusser's critique of this metaphor, in favor of a structure of relatively autonomous instances, is discussed above. I wish only to add a few points in order to make clear my view of the concepts to be employed.

The property connection (or relations of production) implies a certain type of development of the productive forces, that is, of the real appropriation connection. Without this transformation of the productive forces, the relations of production cannot develop. For example, the capitalist mode of production is defined as a double separation of laborers from the means of production, a separation by property (the laborer owns only labor power) and by real appropriation as well (the direct producer cannot initiate the production process on her/his own). Thus, without the separation of workers from the means of production being brought about by mechanization, labor power cannot circulate as commodity, and capitalist property relations can lead only a purely formal existence. Furthermore, not only do capitalist relations *require* such a transformation of the forces of production; to the extent that they are dominant, they *cause* this development as well. Specifically, the action of capitalists, in raising the rate of surplus value, is what revolutionizes the forces of production; therefore, the tendency toward such a development already exists in the capitalist mode of production.

But this correspondence between the forces and relations of production involves another correspondence between capitalist relations of production and the legal and ideological forms in which these relations are expressed. Capitalist relations imply that certain functions be performed by these superstructures; and, again, capitalism cannot develop unless these functions are performed. The wage-labor relation requires the expression of the relations of production in the ratios at which commodities are exchanged which in turn requires some system of legal contracts.

It is this correspondence, between the relations of production and their legal, ideological expression, which the base-superstructure metaphor is meant to capture, although it does so inadequately. In short, some sort of base-superstructure relationship within the relations of production is present in all modes of production.[50] Although dissimulation is a relationship within the property connection, it is determined by the specific articulation of the relations of production with the productive forces. In the capitalist mode of production, a double separation of the direct producer from the means of production exists; the laborer owns no means of production and the forces of production develop in such a way as to remove the control of the labor process from the hands of workers. Labor power is reunited with the means of production only insofar as it circulates as a commodity, only insofar, that is, as it is expressed in a legal form is it rendered equivalent to other factors of production. The labor process thus appears as a putting together of various factors (all commodities) under the direction of capital. That is to say, the labor process appears as a capacity of capital. In sum, the particular dissimulation determined by the specific articulation of the forces and relations of production in capitalism results in an ideological joining of the two.

In other modes of production, for example in the feudal mode of production, this joining does not occur.[51] There, surplus labor is extracted in the form of rent, and the rent relation is guaranteed by the existence of landed property and by enforcement of the landlord's right of exclusion. The separation of the direct producer from the means of production is, therefore, of a different type. Consequently, while in capitalism the fetishization of the economic instance results in an ideological joining of the forces and relations of production, in the feudal mode of production it is the political instance which is fetishized, which appears as natural and eternal. That is, the rent relation is backed up by force, but it appears as a system of relations of personal dependence. Moreover, the labor process does not appear as a power of landlords.

The general concept of fetish outlined here is not assimilable to the architectural metaphor of society, for this concept hinges upon an entry of superstructural elements directly into the economic base.

Bearing these refinements in mind, I should conclude by stating that the methodology employed here is Structuralist. That is to say, I will identify empiricism, and the methodological approaches based on empiricism, as a form of ideology. Where, for example, an approach to the analysis of transition is shown to rest upon epistemological assumptions characterized by an opposition/connection between subject and object, it can be rejected. In addition, I will employ several of Althusser's key concepts in my analysis: structural causality, dissimulation, and the articulation of the relations with the forces of production.

MODES OF PRODUCTION

In this section, I will outline Balibar's approach to a general theory of modes of production. As noted by Balibar, a lack of consistency exists between Marx's treatment of the capitalist mode of production, from which a general theory of modes of production is to be derived, and his treatment of precapitalist modes of production. I will take Marx's analysis of the capitalist mode of production to be the best model for a general theory of modes of production. By the same token, the conventional Marxist approach to feudalism, which is based upon comments made by Marx on the feudal mode of production, will be treated as an error.[52]

The process of constructing a theory of modes of production involves generalizing from Marx's analysis of the capitalist mode of production, even where such generalizations conflict (as they often do) with Marx's remarks on other modes of production. For example, Balibar argues that

Marx inadequately separates the concepts of relations and forces of production in his work on precapitalist modes of production, and that this error is due to a false generalization of the specific forms of these connections between capitalist and precapitalist modes of production.[53]

Any mode of production, for Balibar, is a specific combination of three elements: laborer, means of production (object and means of labor) and nonlaborer. However, any such combination is defined by two relations, or connections, between the elements involved: a property connection and a real appropriation connection.[54] It is clear that Balibar wishes to generalize a concept that appears again and again in Marx's discussion of the capitalist mode of production: the division of labor, social and material. In the analysis of the capitalist mode of production, this duality is seen in the distinction between the production of value and of use-values, and in the ownership of the product of labor as opposed to control over the labor process. That is, these connections correspond to what are traditionally referred to, respectively, as the relations and forces of production.

The capitalist mode of production is defined by a particular double connection/separation of the laborer from the means of production. In terms of the property connection, the laborer holds no property (except labor power). At the same time, the labor is separated from any ability to set in motion the means of production. This second sense in which the laborer is separated from the means of production, which refers to the real appropriation connection, is associated with the loss of craft skill and the development of modern machinery. However, the fact that, under capitalism, both relations can be described as a separation of the laborer from the means of production, leads Marx into error in his characterization of precapitalist modes of production. Therefore, the concept of feudalism upon which much of the work on the transition to capitalism is based, and the one which, quite clearly, Marx suggested, constitutes a (false) generalization. Thus, Marx characterized feudalism as a mode of production in which the laborer is not separated from the means of production. As a result, the extraction of surplus labor cannot occur economically, but is rather portrayed as a result of political domination and servitude.[55] Feudalism is also identified with one type of rent only: labor rent (serfdom). However, we shall see below that the feudal mode of production is more usefully defined in terms of a particular economic separation of the direct producer from the means of production, that this separation is based on the existence of landed property, and that surplus labor is extracted from direct producers in the form of rent, whether rent is rendered in labor, production, or in money.

In sum, the approach to the feudal mode of production dominating Marxist discussion of this topic, a concept of feudalism as a nonseparation of the direct producer from the means of production, is (1) inconsistent with Marx's treatment of the capitalist mode of production in *Capital*, and (2) incompatible with a general theory of modes of production based on Marx's treatment of the capitalist mode of production.

THE TRANSITION TO CAPITALISM

The question central to discussion in this section is at what level of abstraction is the transition to capitalism to be theorized. An important difference exists among Structuralist writers on this point. Balibar argues that the transition should be analyzed as a mode of production. Bettleheim, on the other hand, treats transitions as social formations. The difference between these two approaches, as I will expand upon below, lies mainly in the degree to which the outcome of the transition is guaranteed.

In the appendix to *Reading Capital*, Althusser describes Marx's project in *Capital* as a delineation of the concept of the specific differences of the capitalist mode of production from other modes of production.[56] Thus, in studying English capitalism, Marx abstracts from the existence of other modes of production in England and gives us no theory of the transition from one mode of production to another. Yet it is precisely such a theory that is needed to solve the problems posed by the so-called "underdeveloped" countries of the Third World.[57] That is, the solution to the problem of development must be found by posing the question of transition as a theoretical problem, and underdeveloped countries are simply not special cases of normal capitalist development.

Charles Bettelheim meets this difficulty by moving to a level of abstraction (called a social formation) in which elements of several modes of production coexist, and in which the relations among different modes of production are the central focus of attention. He contrasts social formation in which a mode of production is dominant to transitional social formations. In transitional social formations, the domination by a single mode of production has been broken "without the possibility of this rupture being followed by such a weakening of the social conditions characteristic of another mode of production that their disappearance can be assured."[58] However, the dominance of a mode of production is a product of the correspondence of its relations. When the elements of a mode of production are in correspondence, they form a complex structure, "the elements of which are reciprocally causes and effects of each other or are supported by one another."[59] In this case, the expanded reproduction of the social relations of such a mode of production entails the dissolution of other types of social relations; that is, that particular mode of production is dominant.

It is noteworthy that Bettelheim extends the delimitation of the transitional social formation beyond the relatively simple introduction of survivals of other modes of production into the analysis suggested by Althusser. The difference is that, for Althusser, all social formations contain dominant modes of production that tend to dissolve (however slowly) the survivals of other modes of production, while for Bettelheim, forms of transition can exist in which no mode is dominant. Consider Bettelheim's only developed example of a transitional form, state capitalism, in which capitalist production relations are articulated within state property. For Bettelheim, the existence of capitalist relations of production does not imply the existence of the capitalist mode of production, since a mode of production only exists if an ensemble of *corresponding* social relations exist simultaneously. Class struggle takes the form of suppression and transformation of the market by the state, without which restoration is guaranteed. That is to say, the state has the power to bring about dramatic alterations in the structure of production. To the extent that the state is controlled by the working class, it will use this power to diminish the influence of the market upon the economy. It will strive, ultimately, to replace commodity categories with the categories of the plan, in which products are distributed as use values. On the other hand, where the bourgeoisie controls the state apparatus, central planning will become an ideological doubling of value relations established by the action of capitalists (the directors of enterprises).

Balibar explicitly criticizes the practice of locating transitions at the level of the social formation. However, as we see below, this is because he identifies the distinction between mode of production/social formation with that between theory and reality.[60] Balibar aims his critique at an empiricist interpretation of modes of production, for which such modes are models of reality. In his view, *Capital* is a study of the properties of the model, the capitalist mode of production, properties that are valid for every case of capitalism in history (e.g., the U.S. in 1988). The application of such models to reality is itself an atheoretical act. That is to say, armed with the properties of this model, the historian is able to decide, from an examination of (empirical) history, which periods are best described by the capitalist mode of production, which are not, and which require the employment of two modes of production, conceived to be in succession.

This interpretation is allegedly supported by survivals of empiricism in Marx.

This does not prevent the same economic basis—the same form from the standpoint of its main conditions—due to innumerable different empirical circumstances, natural environment, racial relations, external historical influences, etc., from showing infinite variations and gradations in appearance, which can be ascertained *only by analysis of the empirically given* circumstances.[61]

According to the empiricist interpretation, the job of theory is to analyze the main conditions of the capitalist mode of production. The evaluation of the suitability of this model, its location in history, is a task to be discovered by empirical analysis.[62]

Marx, having laid the basis for a theoretical disruption of the ideological continuity of history in order to reconstitute history as a science of discontinuous modes of production, reestablishes (in the passage quoted above) this continuity as a real reference.[63] That is, theory produces models, and the problem of the application of these models is beyond the limits of theory.

Balibar treats the irreducibly empirical residue as a theoretical gap, i.e., something which must be filled if there is to be a science of modes of production, yet cannot be thought in terms of the concept of mode of production alone.[64] According to Balibar, what is required is a concept of transition (the formation and dissolution of modes of production) theorized at the same level of abstraction as mode of production. This approach is opposed to that of searching through history for the location of the capitalist mode of production. Therefore, Balibar does not analyze the transition at the level of the social formation (in the sense in which he uses the term).

Balibar's project consists, rather, in reading Marx's work on the formation and dissolution of modes of production in order to derive a general concept of transition. A first principle of this task involves *not* treating transitions as concretizations of modes of production. In this manner, the analysis of transitions is distanced from that of social formations, since the latter are "concrete complex wholes . . . at a certain place and stage of development."[65] While I will criticize below the concept of a transitional mode of production, I am nevertheless in agreement with (1) Balibar's critique of the ideology of models, (the empiricist interpretation of Marx described above) and (2) with his attempt to theorize the transition in a nonempiricist manner. My purpose is to investigate the various problems associated with underdevelopment, in the light of a developed concept of the transition from feudalism to capitalism.

CONCLUSION

In this chapter, I have contrasted two approaches to transition to capitalism: Bettelheim's transitional social formation and Balibar's transitional mode of production. In doing so, I have discussed the methodological underpinnings of contemporary work on the transition. In broad agreement with the Structuralist approach, I will employ its principles for the remainder of this book. This means that, in my view, empiricist methodologies are incompatible with a scientific treatment of the transition to capitalism. It does not mean, however, that all of Althusser's and

Balibar's formulations are complete. I have criticized the formulation of last-instance economic determination, and I am in disagreement, for reasons discussed in Chapters 2 and 3, with the idea of a transitional mode of production.

I have defended, on the other hand, Balibar's general theory of modes of production against the criticism of Hindess and Hirst. Such a general theory is, in my view, prerequisite to a theory of transition since it provides a theoretical space in which different modes of production can be situated. And, as we have seen above, a theory of transition presupposes a knowledge of the specific differences between the modes of production from which and to which transition takes place.

Finally, I began discussion on the question of what level of analysis is appropriate to the study of transition, and we have seen that the Structuralists are divided on this question. While I find it necessary to modify Balibar's transitional mode of production, many of the concepts raised in the context of his approach are important in later chapters. Consequently, I proceed, in the following chapter, to a more detailed exposition and critique of the transitional mode of production.

NOTES

1. Rodney Hilton, ed., *The Transition from Feudalism to Capitalism* (London: New Left Books, 1976; Verso Edition, 1978).

2. Confrontation between the British historians and the Structuralists began in earnest with the publication in 1978 of E. P. Thompson's polemic against Althusser, *The Poverty of Theory* (London: New Left Books, 1978). This book constituted an overall attack on the Althusserians, as opposed to the piecemeal critiques and relatively uncontroversial exegeses that had followed immediately upon Althusser's translation into English.

3. Alex Callinicos takes similar approach in *Althusser's Marxism* (London: Pluto Press, 1976). For a treatment of Althusser in relation to non-Marxist structuralists, see Russell Keat and John Urry, *Social Theory as Science* (London: Routledge and Kegan Paul, 1975). Also Goran Therborn, *Science, Class and Society* (London: New Left Books, 1976), for a comparison of Althusserian Marxism to bourgeois social theory.

4. See Perry Anderson's criticism of E. P. Thompson for not mentioning the Sino-Soviet dispute in his critique of Althusser's "Stalinism," in *Arguments Within English Marxism* (London: New Left Books, 1980), p. 106.

5. Louis Althusser, *For Marx* (London: New Left Books, 1977), p. 237.

6. The influence of Mao on Althusser is most visible in "Contradiction and Overdetermination," in *For Marx*, pp. 89–187. Also see Anderson, p. 107.

7. Althusser, "Marxism and Humanism," in *For Marx*, pp. 219–247.

8. Lucio Colletti, *Marxism and Hegel* (London: New Left Books, 1973). Also see Garreth Stedman Jones, "Engels and the End of Classical German Philosophy," *New Left Review*, No. 79 (May–June 1973), pp. 8–26. Also see Callinicos, pp. 10–29.

9. Friedrich Engels, *Dialectics of Nature* (Moscow: International Publishers, 1954).

10. Colletti, p. 50.

11. Althusser includes Gramsci and Colletti, as well as Lukacs, among the historicists. The term, historicism, refers, for Althusser, to any of a variety of views that assimilate knowledge to the self-consciousness of a given moment of time. See Ben Brewster, Glossary to *Reading Capital*, p. 314. Thus, both deriving a knowledge of events from the movement of a central idea through time (as in Hegel) and testing knowledge by reference to an historical present (as in positivist epistemologies of verification or falsification) would qualify as an example of historicism.

12. Georg Lukacs, *History and Class Consciousness* (London: Camelot Press, 1971), pp. 121–122.

13. Callinicos, pp. 20–21.

14. Brewster, p. 313.

15. *Ibid.*, p. 314.

16. Friedrich Engels, *Anti-Duhring* (Moscow: Foreign Language Publishing House, 1962).

17. Callinicos, p. 32.

18. Louis Althusser, "From *Capital* to Marx's Philosophy," in Althusser and Balibar, pp. 52–53.

19. Althusser, *For Marx*, pp. 49–86.

20. Karl Marx and Friedrich Engels, *The German Ideology* (London: International Publishers, 1970).

21. Brewster, p. 318.

22. Althusser, *For Marx*, pp. 87–128.

23. Colletti, pp. 52–67.

24. Structural cause is "nothing outside of its effects." See Althusser and Balibar, *Reading Capital*, p. 189.

25. Callinicos, pp. 51–52, offers a good example of this point.

26. Thompson, p. 374, also see Anderson's defense of Althusser, on this score, in Anderson, pp. 103–112.

27. Althusser and Balibar, *Reading Capital*, p. 43.

28. Thompson, p. 205.

29. *Ibid.*

30. Paul Feyerabend, *Against Method* (Atlantic Highlands, New Jersey: Humanities Press, 1975).

31. Joan Robinson, *Economic Philosophy* (Chicago: Aldine Publishing Company, 1962).

32. Barry Hindess and Paul Hirst, *Pre-Capitalist Modes of Production* (London: Routledge and Kegan Paul, 1975), chapter six.

33. André Glucksmann, "A Ventriloquist Structuralism," *New Left Review*, No. 72 (March–April 1972), pp. 100–160.

34. Callinicos, p. 77.

35. Althusser, *For Marx*, p. 169.

36. Glucksmann, p. 135.

37. Althusser, *Lenin and Philosophy and Other Essays* (London: New Left Books, 1971).

38. Callinicos, p. 88.

39. Etienne Balibar, "On the Basic Concepts of Historical Materialism," in Louis Althusser and Etienne Balibar, *Reading Capital*, pp. 199–308.

40. *Ibid.*, p. 215.

41. Hindess and Hirst, *Pre-Capitalist Modes of Production*, pp. 7–8.

42. Barry Hindess and Paul Hirst, *Mode of Production and Social Formation* (London: Macmillan, 1977).

43. See Brewster, p. 315.

44. Althusser, *For Marx*, pp. 87–128.

45. Charles Bettelheim, *Economic Calculation and Forms of Property* (London: Routledge and Kegan Paul, 1976).

46. Pierre-Phillippe Rey, *Les alliances des classes* (Paris, France: Maspero Press, 1976). In the second essay of this book, Rey is at pains to differentiate himself from Althusser and Balibar, however, his debt to the Marxist-Structuralist school remains large.

47. Marx, 1:81.

48. Maurice Godelier, "Infrastructures, Societies and History," *New Left Review* No. 112 (November–December, 1978), pp. 84–96.

49. *Ibid.*, p. 90.

50. I will refer to this relationship as "dissimulation."

51. Nevertheless, the ideological joining of the forces and relations of production is not unique to capitalism. Marx's remarks on the Asiatic mode of production suggest that the labor process appears as a capacity of the state. See Karl Marx, *Pre-Capitalist Economic Formations* (London: Lawrence and Wishart, 1964), p. 121. Also see Godelier's analysis of the Mbuti Pygmies in Maurice Godelier, *Perspectives in Marxist Anthropology*, trans. Robert Brain (Cambridge: Cambridge University Press, 1977), pp. 51–62.

52. This is the approach taken by the authors of the works compiled by Hilton.

53. Balibar, p. 215.

54. *Ibid.*

55. Marx, *Capital*, 3:790.

56. Althusser and Balibar, *Reading Capital*, p. 196.

57. *Ibid.*, p. 197.

58. Bettelheim, p. 72.

59. *Ibid.*

60. Balibar, p. 300n.

61. Marx, *Capital*, 3:791–92.

62. This interpretation clearly dominates the literature on the transition to capitalism. It is also found in more methodological form among empiricist accounts of Althusser (e.g., Keat and Urry), and it forms the basis of the critique of Balibar found in Hindess and Hirst, pp. 260–87.

63. Balibar, p. 257.

64. *Ibid.*

65. Brewster, p. 313.

4

VALUES, MONEY, AND PRICES IN A THEORETICAL SYNCHRONY

In the chapters that follow we will have occasion to draw a rigorous distinction between *synchronic* and *diachronic* analyses. The capitalist mode of production, or any other, may be considered either "in its own time" (as a synchrony), with its various elements fully developed and functioning to reinforce each other, or in a time characterized by the transition from one mode of production to another (as a diachrony), in which elements from different modes of production coexist. Our goal is to apply the concept of diachrony in more detail to the analysis of economic calculation (price formation in the capitalist mode of production) in developing countries.

It will be first necessary to examine the concepts that have been developed, by Marx, and others, to understand accumulation and economic calculation *synchronically*, i.e., as it appears in the capitalist mode of production. The purpose of the next two chapters, consequently, is to summarize several of the more important concepts associated with economic calculation in capitalism. However, these concepts are frequently presented at quite different levels of abstraction and it is difficult, as a result, to compare them. Our task will therefore involve sorting them out in relation to the various levels of abstraction that Marx employed.

Initially, Marx's argument proceeds on at least two levels: that of appearance, where equals exchange for equals and free exchange provides, by definition, the social framework in which public benefit is maximized; and the social level, where the basis of exchange is formed in class exploitation. Consider, by way of example, Marx's general formula for capital, M-C-M': Capitalists advance variable and constant capital, combine labor power and the means of production, and sell the commodities produced. Each transactor receives a price for his or her commodity, and all is well. The rot in Denmark is revealed by the other side of Marx's analysis, which theorizes a process by which labor power is rendered a commodity and human productive effort transformed into an immense and alien social force, placing one transactor in a relation of subjugation to the other. A central difficulty in much contemporary Marxist economic theory lies in failing to connect concrete data with underlying social causes.

This problem is acute at the level of prices, where the data appear not in the determinate sphere of production but in that of exchange. Our project will be to build up categories of analysis sufficiently robust to explain economic calculation on the basis of changes in the sphere of production, proceeding from abstract value analysis to more complex price categories.

Roughly speaking, Marx analyzed the capitalist mode of production through an integration of four levels of analysis: (1) the production of values (including the alteration of magnitude of value in the development of the productive forces), (2) the circulation of values (largely in abstraction from technical change but with respect to the requirements of simple and extended reproduction), (3) the distribution of surplus value among sectors of capital (static production price formation) and among fractions of the capitalist class (the division of profit into that of enterprise and interest), and (4) the formation of market prices as disequilibrium deviations from prices of production.[1] Contemporary Marxist theories of accumulation tend to fixate at some level of abstraction, identifying that level with concrete reality as such. A consideration of the relationship between accumulation and economic calculation at each level of abstraction will facilitate the understanding of the key concepts. In this chapter, I discuss money and growth in the context of the production of surplus value.

THE PRODUCTION OF SURPLUS VALUE

Any serious attempt to understand accumulation and crisis on the basis of an integration of Marx's theories of value and money will lead to a fundamental discovery: unlike neoclassical and neoRicardian theories of accumulation, which rely crucially on the assumption of a given homogeneous space of representation (utility or labor-time, respectively), a Marxian theory of accumulation must comprehend the rupture between the value of a commodity, the labor socially necessary to produce it, and the expression of this value in the use-value of another commodity for which it is exchanged. As I argue below, the roots of this deviation are to be found in the process of value formation itself. As a result, the particular transformation of the productive forces implied by the development of capitalist production relations brings about a designation of capitalist economic calculation. This, of course, remains to be shown. Our immediate concern is to differentiate theories of accumulation from each other. This is done according to the various levels of analysis at which the implications of this rupture can be demonstrated.

The process of value formation involves the determination of a distribution of social labor that guarantees the reproduction of capitalist relations. Thus, only that portion of individual labor that is socially necessary is validated in the exchange of commodities. Labor is validated where it exchanges for an equivalent quantity of labor expended upon another commodity. If, due to an increase in the average productivity of the labor producing a commodity, superfluous labor is expended in production, that labor is not validated, i.e., does not become social labor. Moreover, even leaving technical change aside, values are formed in perpetual reallocations of social labor; they form gravity centers around which exchange ratios fluctuate.

This static formulation is designed to illustrate the distribution of social labor through the exchange process. While the determination of prices by values can take place only on the basis of developed capitalist production, several of the elements of such production—e.g., uniform profit rate among sectors, accumulation, and technical change—are deliberately absent at this level of abstraction.

While exchange values already involve the expression of the value of a commodity in the use-value of another, values are generally expressed in the capitalist mode of production in terms of one commodity: the category price. Prices, ignoring the distribution of surplus value among sectors according to capital advanced, are proportional to values. The ratio of total price to total value is equal to the inverse of the value of gold (the money commodity).

The time-honored debate over the commodity status of money concerns the distinction between quantity theory of money (for which money can have no value) and the determination of the price level in production. According to Marx, the issue of symbolic money fosters the quantity theory illusion of ideal money. Our only intervention will be to suggest that it is more in line with our general method (and Marx's) to begin with an analysis of a commodity system and proceed to more complex forms, without of course denying that the laws corresponding to the issue of symbolic money (to the extent that this issue is in excess of the supply of gold) differ from the laws of a commodity money system.[2]

For Marx, the amount of money required to circulate is given by the ratio of total price to the velocity of money, where total price is the total value produced relative to the value of gold.[3] An excess supply of gold does not imply an increase in prices, for as money, "the perfect and durable form of wealth,'' gold can and must be withheld from circulation.[4] Thus, simply because a quantity of gold exists does not mean that all of it functions as a means of circulation. We should note that neither inflation nor deflation can occur without either a change in the value of gold or in the level of hoarding; typically, the selling of gold is a function of the pace of accumulation. When this pace quickens, more gold is needed to be advanced as money capital against labor power and the means of production. Only gold sales out of proportion to changes in the accumulation rate could cause money to depreciate. This law applies to the issue of symbolic money as well, so long as that issue does not exceed the supply of gold.

However, in addition to performing the functions mentioned thus far— expression of values and means of circulation—money also serves as well as a functional separation of purchase from sale, the actual unity of which is reasserted in a monetary crisis. The impossibility of selling where no one has bought may become evident in a failure of values to realize, where the validation of individual labors is possible only if the state issues inconvertible notes as means of payment to clear balances. In this manner, the circulation of value continues, although validations of labor no longer correspond to any genuine realization.[5] Credit extended among capitalists to permit the false validation of individual labors becomes inflationary where the debt holder is able to redeem her or his debt for commodities, and that redemption is state sanctioned by the issue of symbolic money in excess of gold supplies. However, complete failure of the realization of values is not a necessary condition for the false validation of individual labors. Technical change may lower the value of a commodity whose owner will nonetheless attempt to validate the individual labor embodied in it. Where credit extension permits this false validation, total value (but not total price) will have fallen, and the existing quantity of symbolic money will have been devalued. In this latter case, the deviation of price from value would be manifest in the constant prices of commodities produced in sectors experiencing rapid technical change.

Several observations about economic calculation and accumulation may be made from the above analysis. Price determination, as distinct from value formation, is an aspect of accumulation in which individual labors are (falsely) validated through manipulations of credit and symbolic money issued by the capitalist state. Such validations do not, in every case, involve rising prices. Finally, not every inflation involves a deviation of price from value. For example, price increases as a result of productivity changes in the gold-mining industry do not involve the false validation of labors.

In a formal sense, state economic activity that reduces the pool of surplus value requires a deviation of price from value, but the *cause* of the deviation is the systematic failure of the capitalist system to produce sufficient surplus value to overcome the growth in the value of constant capital. Most simply, the capitalist state will raise prices in order that individual capitalists can gain the profits they need to expand. Credit, followed ultimately by printing money, facilitates the realization of these prices, allowing capitalists to gain profits by selling at prices greater than value.[6] The ultimate limitation upon such state-induced expansion is that state activity is financed by capital itself (through redistributions of surplus value). Since unproductive labor creates no surplus value, state intervention (except as so far as it assists the production, and not merely the realization, of surplus value, e.g., nationalized industries) reduces profits, finally forcing capitalists to raise prices further. Of course, to the extent that such price increases force a deviation of the wage from the value of labor power, capitalists might recoup their losses through redistribution of value from the working class to capital, but in the capitalist mode of production considered as a synchrony, such a deviation must be temporary and limited. Profits fall, and the crisis finally breaks out, despite all attempts of the state to prevent it through redistributions of surplus value. What is of importance here is that state intervention is a necessary condition for false validation of labors. However, it is equally important to note that government spending is neither a reflection of a state commitment to full employment policies, nor a commitment imposed upon the state by the action of the working class.[7]

State intervention originates in the real subsumption of labor by capital; it is implied by the transformation of productive forces under capitalism. I refer here to the sort of state intervention that is peculiarly capitalist, and not to the role of the state in the transition to capitalism, which, as an aspect of the articulation of two modes of production, is out of the range of the current discussion. In formal subsumption, the operation of the law of value establishes a single price in each sector to that which is socially necessary. However, it is only once the capitalist mode of production attains the level of correspondence referred to as real subsumption, in which the forces of production are developed in a capitalist manner, i.e., systematically freed from any but a market connection to the direct producer, that the law of value distributes the expenditures of labor toward the more productive branches of production. This distribution of social labor is subject to and modified by the distribution of surplus value to different sectors according to capital advanced.

To the extent that labor is thus socialized, however, the value form is designified. The value form itself displays important limitations in the degree to which the operation of its law establishes a distribution of social labor ensuring the expanded reproduction of capitalist production relations. Moreover, this designification of the value form can show up as a contradiction between the required distribution of social labor and the distribution of labor expenditures determined by the operation of the law of value. This is a direct result of the socialization of the productive forces, in which the overall social effects of a particular expenditure of labor are not reflected in the value produced by such labor.[8] Examples include certain industries (transportation, electricity) which, by their operation, enable vast reductions in the labor time socially necessary to produce other commodities as well as expenditures of unproductive labor (e.g., education, scientific research) that create no surplus value, but allow its expanded production in other sectors. The greater the socialization of labor, the more centralized the forces of production, the more important this designification of the value form becomes.

The nature of capitalist state intervention in the formation of prices, through subsidies, credit extension, and price fixing is based on the inability on the part of any individual capital to defy the law of value. This applies as much to phenomena similar to the Factory Acts, in which the price of labor was fixed, as to government subsidization of scientific research.

The important point is that state intervention is a necessity of capitalist expansion, and not a mechanism designed to let capitalists cheat the crisis of realization. Furthermore, the function of unproductive state expenditure is not primarily to aid in the realization of existing surplus value (although it may have that effect), but to enable the expansion of the circuits of capital.

The formal requirement for the quasi-autonomous role of the state with regard to economic calculation is the issuance of symbolic money. For, in the commodity money case, any alteration in the quantity of the means of circulation can only be affected through the hoarding mechanism. Those same forces leading to an increase in the pace of accumulation (shown principally in rising profit rates) also call forth the hoards. If, due to technical change or an insufficient accumulation rate, the total value of commodity capital is not commensurate with the existing quantity of money capital, then hoarding must occur to withdraw money capital from circulation. But, under the conditions of symbolic money issuance, it is possible to lower the purchasing power of the existing means of circulation through an expansion of the symbolic money supply.[9]

The advance of credit (as money capital), either in order to expand the circuits of capital or as means of payment to ease a recession, presupposes that surplus value will be produced and realized, if not, then either currency must be devalued or the hoards be swollen if money capital is to be advanced to cover variable and constant capital.

Credit, as money capital, is essential to the accumulation process, For, without it centralization (the reduction in the number of capitals in a sector) and concentration (the internal growth of a given capital) are limited by the quantity of realized surplus value. With inflation, accumulation can proceed, if not without limit then at least without the same periodic growth in hoards. Moreover, the distribution of credit, in such a way as to allow for the expansion of capitalist relations of production, requires state intervention. And, this requirement becomes more severe in proportion to the development of the forces of production in capitalism. Money prices are thus determined in the interplay of the lowering of values (by technical change), the rate of accumulation, and the growth (or shrinkage) of hoards, where each of these factors are altered by the intervention of the state in the process of production.

CONCLUSION

In this chapter, I have discussed money and economic growth in the context of the production of surplus value in the capitalist mode of production, considered as a synchrony. The central conclusion is that a theory of economic calculation in the capitalist mode of production must account for the rupture between value and its expression in exchange rates. Thus, the role of the capitalist state is brought in as the institutional guarantor of social reproduction. Finally, the relative importance of the state increases with the evolution of the capitalist mode of production.

NOTES

1. B. Fine and L. Harris, *Rereading Capital* (New York: Columbia University Press, 1979), chapter one.

2. John Weeks, *Capital and Exploitation* (Princeton, New Jersey: Princeton University Press, 1981), p. 16.

3. Marx, *Capital*, 1:17.

4. *Ibid.*, p. 134.

5. Suzanne de Brunhoff, *Les rapports d'argent* (Grenoble: Presses Universitaires de Grenoble, 1979), pp. 120–35.

6. D. Yaffe, "The Crisis of Profitability: A Critique of the Glyn-Sutcliffe Thesis," *New Left Review*, No. 80 (1973), p. 46.

7. Yaffe, p. 54.

8. Charles Bettelheim, *Economic Calculation*, p. 42.

9. Fine and Harris, p. 180. Also see Jean-Luc Dallemagne, "L'Inflation et crises ou le mythe de la 'stagflation,' " *Critiques de l'economie politique* (Paris: Francois Maspero, 1974), p. 167.

5

DISTRIBUTION AND ACCUMULATION IN A SYNCHRONY

In this chapter, I consider economic calculation in the context of the distribution of surplus value, both among sectors of production and between fractions of the capitalist class. Also discussed are the formation of wages and accumulation.

THE DISTRIBUTION OF SURPLUS VALUE

In the production of value, the crucial variable is the rate of exploitation. The quantity of surplus value (that quantity of living labor expended in production above that required to reproduce the working class) at a given level of productivity is in class struggle determined by the length of the working day and the intensity of the production process. However, the rate of exploitation can be increased relatively by raising the productivity of the labor that produces (directly or indirectly) wage goods.

The distribution of surplus value takes place, however, on the basis of equal returns to capital (constant and variable) advanced, i.e., on the basis of the establishment of a general rate of profit among sectors of production. Formally, this distribution principle necessitates a deviation of what is called the price of production from the exchange value of the commodity.

As a result of the distribution of surplus value, origins of surplus value (in unpaid living labor) are hidden by the calculation of profit on total capital advanced; just as all traces of individual labors are effaced in their expression in the value form, here all differences between the quantities of value produced between sectors are obliterated.[1] Consequently, the value of output appears to be divided among profits and wages.

Marx's method of showing the deviation of production prices from exchange values, given this distribution principle, has been criticized in numerous places, and we shall not come to its defense except to note that a formal solution to the difficulties associated with the transformation of inputs has long been available.[2] It involves rewriting Marx's transformation procedure as a set of n simultaneous equations with $n +$ 2 unknowns (the n prices, the wage rate, and the rate of profit). This system can be reduced to a single degree of freedom by specifying the ratio of the price rate of profit to the wage rate. This formal property of the solution has given rise to the notion of an independent determination of income distribution (the profit-wage ratio) in class struggle, as opposed to considering the wage to be a determinate deviation from the value of labor power.[3]

In theories of economic calculation and accumulation, this focus on distribution has led to conflicting theories in which class struggle over resources determines the profit-wage ratio.[4] In this scenario, union militancy causes wages to pinch profits, which can precipitate a crisis or, depending on the degree of monopoly, can push prices up. Unions respond to the negative effect of inflation on the real wage by further wage demands, and so on.

A second strand of analysis based on distribution is the administered price thesis. When considered at the level of static production price formation, monopoly consists of barriers to the establishment of prices of production, and monoply price is a redistribution of surplus value. The process of centralization, however, depending as it does upon technical change, of which monopoly is but the result, is necessarily absent. The error of discussing monopoly price in a static framework leads so quickly to its (stagnationist) conclusions that we need only examine the argument briefly.[5]

With competition (defined not in terms of technical change or intersectoral relationships, but simply as the inability to affect market price by output decisions) eliminated in many sectors, monopoly price (a special case of market price) is established. Monopoly price is greater than production price and monopoly profit is greater than average profit, and therefore greater than profits in the competitive sector.[6] Small capital is deenergized by low profits, and large capital avoids technical change, complacently allowing its high monopoly profit rate to protect the value of its fixed capital.

Falling profits in the competitive sector will force price increases there too, as small capital attempts to pass on the squeeze to the working class. Where the working class defends the real wage, money wages must rise. Consequently, small capital feels its profits squeezed by rising wage and/or capital goods cost. Sherman finds (in respect to the U.S.) that during the expansion the working class is not able to keep the real wage constant so that the burden of monopoly profits falls upon both workers and small capitalists.[7]

The theoretical separation of centralization from the sphere of production, thus treating it as a distribution phenomena, gives the misleading impression that monopolies of necessity inhibit accumulation. While this is certainly true under certain circumstances, what those circumstances are is not ascertainable without explicit consideration of (Marxian) competition. Moreover, what data like that of Sherman show is the centralization process as it appears: as a fight over market shares that ultimately reduces competition in some sectors, leading to further centralization as crises take their toll on small capital. What such data, as they stand, do not show is the competitive struggle between capital and labor over technical change in the production process. This struggle determines deviations of the wage from the value of labor power as well as the quantity of profit produced. To discuss centralization properly, a category of disequilibrium excess profits (a redistribution of surplus value within a given sector, not equivalent to monopoly profit) available to innovating capitals is necessary. As a final point on centralization, it is wrong to think of monopoly prices as any sort of misallocation of labor expenditures, since, as we say in the previous section, the distribution of social labor determined by the law of value is already in contradiction to the smooth reproduction of capitalist production relations, and this contradiction stems not from the number of firms in an industry but from the socialization of labor. In the case of an industry employing a quantity of fixed capital, in which is embodied not only the labor time socially necessary to produce this machinery but a high degree of scientific knowledge, developed in the interest of but at no cost to capital, the price of production defined by the average rate of profit will neither be determined by all the labor time socially necessary to produce this product, nor will it distribute sufficient quantities of social labor toward industries with overall social effects. The effect of deviation of market price from such a production price on accumulation cannot be ascertained in an a priori manner.

The distribution of surplus value among fractions of the capitalist class, especially the division of profits into profit of enterprise and interest payments, provides the framework for a discussion of interest-bearing capital and credit. Recall that credit as money capital is extended as part of the centralization process and that where, as a result, total value falls (due to technical change and an insufficient compensating increase in the accumulation rate), this expansion of credit is inflationary. This general statement of the relationship between credit and centralization is not meant to imply that, at times, the advance of credit will not serve inefficient firms, and thus inhibit centralization. The demand for money capital, according to Marx, is especially sharp during recessions as payments fall due.[8] Credit extension is ultimately a redistribution of surplus value from industrial to interest-bearing capital, but it is a redistribution that has the effect of allowing surplus value to be created.

In sum, when the distribution of surplus value among branches of capital is brought into consideration, the possibility exists for an explanation of economic calculation based on the exogenous determination of the distribution of income. To the extent that classes compete with one another in this respect, an increase in wages may lead capitalists to push up prices to maintain the profit-wage ratio. However, we have criticized this approach where it is not based on a determination of wages and profits in production. Furthermore, we have outlined the administered price theory and criticized it for treating centralization as a phenomenon isolated from the sphere of production.

THE FORMATION OF WAGES

The possibility of a long-term deviation of the price of labor from the value of labor power would seem to be limited in a synchronic analysis of capitalism, because such an analysis presupposes the reproduction of the conditions of existence of the mode of production. The limits of this variation are analyzed by Marx through the concept of market price.

Production prices provide gravity centers around which market prices fluctuate as a result of (ceaseless) sectoral imbalances. Thus, market price will exceed production prices in some sectors and fall below them in others; likewise, the sales rate of profit will not equal the general rate of profit (although sales profits are limited by general profits). Capital movements will result from such disequilibrium, which will tend to re-equilibrate production prices and market prices. This process is important when considered in conjunction with technical change.

More immediately, such a framework allows for temporary deviations of the wage from the value of labor power and, therefore, for redistribution of value from the working class to capital, although these redistributions are held within strict limits by the requirements of social reproduction. Some writers have placed considerable importance on this property, implying that capital uses inflation to raise the rate of surplus value.[9] Mandel goes so far as to suggest that inflation is a substitute for the reserve army (keeping wages down in times of full employment, so long as the banking system cooperates by expanding the money supply). Glyn and Sutcliffe make essentially the same argument, although they seem to have less faith in capital's ability to avoid the squeeze by putting up prices.[10] A great deal depends upon the limits to the deviation of wages from the value of labor power (limits which the cost-push problematic tends to ignore, as seen in the previous section). Furthermore, when the cost-push problematic is confronted with technical change, some of its conclusions seem less sure. In order for wages to systematically pinch profits, the pace of accumulation must place sufficient pressure upon the labor market to compensate for falling production prices of wage goods and the expulsion of living labor from the production process (which tends to swell the reserve army and drive down wages). Nonetheless, the deviation of wages from the value of labor power plays an important role in centralization, putting wage-push pressure on inefficient capitals.

MONEY AND GROWTH

The difficulty, as seen above, with the administered price thesis is that it considers the formation of a special market price (monopoly price) as a barrier to the establishment of a general rate of profit, given a certain technique of production, without reflecting upon those barriers resulting from past technical change. For Marx, competition is not *generally* limited by the degree of centralization in a sector of production, for competition is (1) dynamic, taking place through technical change, and (2) intersectoral (because technical change in one sector may introduce competitiveness into another). Both the depth of technical change and the response of prices to technical changes are influenced by credit as means of payment, and, therefore, by state intervention.

Technical change is a disequilibrating force in which some of the individual labor expended upon wage goods and upon the means of production loses its social character; it is not validated in the exchange of commodities because commodities, generally, are realized at lower values.

An effect upon the price rate of profit will be exercised by the increase in the technical composition that accompanies technical change (an increase in the mass of machinery set into motion by a worker). As is well known from the large variety of critiques of Marx's law of the tendency of the rate of profit to fall, the effect on profits will depend upon the actual formation of market prices, i.e., upon whether or not they fall to the production prices implied by the new technique.[11] Credit appears to act on both sides of this process. The extension of credit as capital works to expand the basis of concentration and centralization beyond the limits of the quantity of realized surplus value. Therefore, given a rate of accumulation, an increase in credit will allow for greater increases in productivity, tending to drive values further downward. Of course, the extension of credit as means of payment may be necessary so that validation of the labor expended in the production of the inputs to production requires not merely that commodities exchange but exchange at market prices greater than the production price implied by the new technique. Credit cannot systematically bring this about, although its advance can ensure that market prices will tend to gravitate around (falling) production prices.

Of course, monopolized sectors can, in principle and for a limited time, keep monopoly prices above implicit production prices, by restricting investment in an effort to amortize fixed capital (just as they can avoid technical change for the same reason). However, the propensity of centralization to place restrictions on technical change is weakened by the lowering of values in other sectors.

The stimulus to competition (understood in Marx's sense) is the availability of excess profits to the innovating capitals (through the reduction of costs). Thus, competition establishes profit rate differentials within sectors. In the static theory of competition (see the previous section), production prices are formed relative to a given technique, i.e., given a value composition of capital. In the case under consideration, technical change raises the technical composition of capital, but its effect on the value composition depends precisely on the formation of prices. It is nevertheless wise to note that, given an alteration in value composition, monopoly price formation can block the establishment of the general rate of profit, but the resultant redistribution of surplus value among branches does not raise surplus value, nor does it alter profit rate differentials within sectors (and thus it does not necessarily inhibit centralization).

CONCLUSION

Price formation depends upon the level of hoarding, since where symbolic money is issued in excess of commodity money, an alteration in the purchasing power of these symbols can equilibrate the money capital to the value of commodity capital, for a given rate of accumulation. Hoarding continues to play an important role, though hoarding of symbolic money lessens as inflation increases. The principal influence upon money prices at the level of state activity is the extension of state credit (backed up by increases in the supply of money) as money capital to facilitate centralization of capital. Moreover, the intervention of the state in the economy is a necessity for the expanded reproduction of capitalism in its advanced form, and the importance of the state sector increases with the development of the forces of production. Consequently, it is this advanced transformation of the productive forces, and the implied economic role of the state, which cause a tendency toward price inflation in advanced capitalism. This tendency is limited and counterbalanced by the development of the forces of production, especially the production of relative surplus value. Note that, under certain conditions, credit extension can inhibit centralization and, therefore, working-class resistance to the effects of centralization can take the form of a demand to expand credit as capital.

Whether or not the quantity of money capital is excessive depends upon the accumulation process, upon the depth of technical change, and upon the portion of surplus value thrown back into production. So long as accumulation proceeds at a pace fast enough to confront money capital with an equivalent *total* value of commodity capital (despite falling unit values), no devaluation of symbolic money is necessary. Where this equivalence is disrupted (which can occur through a fall in the rate of accumulation *or* by rapid technical change accompanied by an insufficiently increasing rate of accumulation), the demand for money capital will expand.

NOTES

1. Susan Himmelweit and Simon Mohun, "The Anomalies of Capital," *Capital and Class*, 6 (August 1978), p. 78.

2. Francis Seton, "The 'Transformation Problem,' " *Review of Economic Studies* 24 (1957): 149–60.

3. Ian Steedman, *Marx After Sraffa* (London: New Left Books, 1977).

4. J. Harvey, "Theories of Inflation," *Marxism Today* 21 (January 1977): 24–28.

5. Hilferding, *Finance Capital* (Boston: Routledge & Kegan Paul, 1981); Howard Sherman, "Inflation, Unemployment and Monopoly Capital," *Monthly Review* 27 (1975): 25–35; Paul Sweezy, "Varieties of Inflation," *Monthly Review* 30 (1978): 44–49.

6. S. Koshimura, *Theory of Capital Reproduction and Accumulation*, ed. Jesse Schwartz, trans. Toshihira Ataka (Kitchener, Canada: DPG Publishing Co., 1975), pp. 128–60.

7. Sherman, pp. 31–33.

8. Laurence Harris, "On Interest Credit and Capital," *Economy and Society* No. 15 (May 1976): 145–77.

9. Ernest Mandel, *Late Capitalism* (London: New Left Books, 1975), p. 270.

10. Andrew Glyn and Robert Sutcliffe, *British Capital, Workers, and the Profits Squeeze* (London: Penguin, 1972), p. 180.

11. John Weeks, *Capital and Exploitation* (Princeton, New Jersey: Princeton University Press, 1981), p. 110.

6

THE THEORY OF NONCORRESPONDENCE

The purpose of this chapter and the next is to outline Balibar's concept of a transitional mode of production. This concept yields many insights, and it is defended, in this chapter, against empiricist criticism. In this chapter, I will review some of the theoretical tools developed in Balibar's discussion of the transitional mode of production.

The first section analyzes the noncorrespondence (or dislocation) between the relations of production and the legal and ideological forms in which these relations appear. Specifically, capitalist legal relations precede the full development of capitalist production relations, so that precapitalist relations may be expressed in capitalist legal and ideological forms. In the second section, I will discuss another dislocation characterizing transitions—that between the forces and relations of production. This dislocation is referred to as formal subsumption, and because no mechanization of the labor process takes place under these conditions, capital's ability to raise the rate of surplus value is limited to absolute means. The key differences between manufacture and modern industry are discussed, and Marx's concept of socialized labor is introduced.

NONCORRESPONDENCE BETWEEN LEVELS

Here I will investigate two examples of noncorrespondence between the relations of production and the legal forms taken by these relations. One involves the distinction between the property connection and the law of property discussed by Balibar. The other is the expression of capitalist production relations in the socialist legal form of property, examined by Bettelheim in his study of the transition to socialism.

Balibar discusses the distinction within the property connection between base and superstructure within the property connection, that is, dislocations between property and its legal expression (the law of property), are characteristic of transitional periods. As an example, Balibar points to the Factory Acts. The idea is that, while the capitalist mode of production implies an economic determination of the rate of exploitation, these acts constituted a political intervention and determination which, as it turns out, played a crucial role in the transition from manufacture to modern industry.

Following this example of discordance, Balibar goes on to seek out the specific distinction between property and the law of property in capitalism. Legal forms, he argues, both express and conceal economic relations, but this should not be taken to mean that specific combinations of elements produce (in the sense of a genesis) a specific legal system. Rather, each combination implies a necessary function of the legal system (Balibar has us recall that the capitalist mode of production makes use of a reactivation of Roman law). Therefore, we are analyzing the articulation of two relatively autonomous levels, of which the economic is logically the prior. The capitalist legal system involves both a law of property (that is, a relation of a person to a thing) and a law of contract (a relation between persons), both of which are *abstract universalistic* in character (anything, for example, can be owned by anybody). This is a condition for the constitution of the capitalist mode of production as a set of elements distributed entirely as commodities and exchangers (as things and persons). The difference between property as a production relation and the law of property is that, in the former case, the only significant property is the means of production, while no legal distinction is made between persons and things. It is likewise true for the law of contract, here a labor contract. Legally, the nature of the labor is irrelevant, but, in so far as we speak of production relations, property consists in the power to consume labor power productively. In both cases, the legal form involves an extension into generality. Note that two forms (law of property and law of contract) have become one property connection and also that, while law defines subjects as individuals, a production relation defines agents by their function in the production process, i.e., as social classes.

For Bettelheim, as for Balibar, noncorrespondence is characteristic of transition. Of course, Bettelheim's most developed example of this is nationalization of the means of production (a legal form of property) as opposed to the socialization of the mode of production (socialist form of property: expropriation of the entire property-owning class). Such a noncorrespondence (here between property and a legal form of property) places limits on the type of development of the forces of production; these limits are the effect of new production relations (here socialist—in the form of the domination of the enterprise by the state). Likewise, noncorrespondence is seen in limits placed upon the legal intervention (here by a workers' state) as a result of the existence of capitalist relations of production. Balibar's insistence on the logical priority of property over the law of property, i.e., of base over superstructure, returns in the notion that in the absence of political intervention, property will exercise dominance over the legal form of this property (here the enterprise is spontaneously dominated by capitalist production relations and a tendency toward the decomposition of state property becomes a part of the laws of motion vis-à-vis the transition).

In so far as the capitalist legal system is displaced by a socialist legal form of property, the effects of the contradictions of capitalism (based as they are on that between the private property and the social character of production) are displaced onto this (new) legal form (here state property). For instance, such effects of crisis as layoffs may appear as a planned movement of workers from one industry to another, a planned movement that requires a certain amount of time.

Whether the new form of property is merely a legal form onto which the contradictions of the old mode of production are displaced, or the means through which the new property form is itself instituted as the property connection, depends on the extent to which this legal form corresponds to the new production relations that can come to dominate the old relations (here it depends on the relation of the workers to the state). This domination (of the old by the new relations) denotes that the reproduction of these old relations no longer determines the fundamental character of the reproduction and transformation of the connections.

From these examples of dislocation, one can draw the following conclusions. (1) The relations of production imply a function to be performed by the legal expression of these relations, but they do not produce a specific legal system. In the capitalist mode of production, for example, the ideology of generalized commodity production presupposes an abstract universalistic legal system. (2) In a transition, a relationship of mutual limitation exists between the production relations of one mode and the legal and ideological relations of another. For example, the existence of capitalist relations of production in the transition to socialism limits the degree of state intervention in the economy, and, therefore, limits the development of socialist relations. (3) The contradictions of one mode of production may be displaced onto the legal forms characteristic of another mode. In a transition to socialism, for example, a tendency for prices to rise may appear as a shortage of certain products.

NONCORRESPONDENCE BETWEEN CONNECTIONS

In this section, I will discuss the formal subsumption of the laborer to capital as a noncorrespondence between capitalist relations of production and the forces of production, which are still of the character of manufacture. However, we see that the chronological dislocation between forces and relations is suppressed in an analysis restricted to the capitalist mode of production. Rather, this dislocation appears as a tendency, in the capitalist mode of production, toward the replacement of manual by mechanized labor. Finally, I will turn to a discussion of Marx's concept of socialized labor. Labor is only socialized where the forces are those of modern industry, in which the labor process is independent of the knowledge and experience of the worker.

Balibar believes that a central tenet of Marxism is the concept of a necessary correlation between certain productive forces and certain types of society (i.e., a necessary correspondence between connections). Thus, capitalist property (specifically as a result of the accumulation process) imposes on the forces of production a type of development peculiar to this form of property. This type of development consists of a specific transformation of the real appropriation connection generally referred to as mechanization. Mechanization is the form of the real appropriation connection organically belonging to the capitalist mode of production.[1]

However, capital initially subordinates labor on the basis of technical conditions given by historical development (hence, absolute surplus value production). Consequently, under the conditions referred to as formal subsumption (as opposed to the real subsumption of labor to capital in fully developed capitalism), certain dislocations occur. First, a *chronological dislocation* occurs in the formation of the different elements of the structure: capital as a social relation exists before real subsumption. Secondly, the process of mechanization (considered in time) is dislocated from one branch to another (first one branch and then another is mechanized).

An extremely important point must be raised here. According to Balibar, the conceptualization of such dislocations is to be done in a theory of synchrony in which the concept of a mode of production is given.[2] This synchrony suppresses the aspect of temporality. As a result, the chronological dislocations mentioned above are suppressed. A second result is that the successive replacement (within a single industry) of manual by mechanized labor, "in a rhythm subject to structural and conjunctural economic necessities," appears as a structural property of the capitalist mode of production (i.e., as a tendency): the "essence of the productive forces in the capitalist mode of production is to be constantly in the process of transition from manual to mechanized labor."[3]

The difference between manufacture (as radicalized handicrafts), and modern industry, is as follows. Manufacture consists of a unity of labor power and the means of labor: the tool must be adapted to the human organism and a tool is only a tool if the laborer knows how to use it. Modern industry is constituted by a unity of the means of labor and the object of labor: the machine tool is adapted to the object of labor and it is independent of the knowledge of the worker. It should be noted that the fundamental theoretical point of Balibar's argument is just that the nature of the elements are transformed along with the connection. Thus, the collective worker is a different individual from the artisan in that her/his mastery over the tool is transformed into a social mastery over nature, i.e., through intellectual labor. All of this makes up Marx's concept of *socialized labor*. Once labor is socialized, an explanation of the labor necessary to produce a commodity requires considering each labor process as an element of social production as a whole. The intellectual labor necessary to the production process (since it is free to capital) is left out of the value of the product, yet it must appear in an analysis of the technical division of the labor process, since laborers are involved who are not at the workplace. I will return below to the notion of socialized labor.

CONCLUSION

In sum, I have argued that the formal subsumption of labor by capital represents a case of noncorrespondence between the forces and relations of production, and that this noncorrespondence cannot be analyzed synchronically in relation to the capitalist mode of production. Furthermore, we have seen that the socialization of labor requires a transformation of the forces of production during the transition from manufacture to modern industry.

NOTES

1. Etienne Balibar, "On the Basic Concepts of Historical Materialism," in Althusser and Balibar, *Reading Capital*, p. 236.
2. *Ibid*.
3. *Ibid*., p. 237.

7

THE TRANSITIONAL MODE OF PRODUCTION

In this chapter, I will investigate two of Marx's approaches to the subject of the transition to capitalism: primitive accumulation and the "tendency of the capitalist mode of production." In the first approach, the development of the elements of the capitalist mode of production are analyzed in abstraction from the structure of the mode of production in which those elements developed. In the second, the structure of the mode of production defines its tendency, but this tendency is toward reproduction, not supersession.

In addition, in this chapter Balibar's crucial distinction between synchrony and diachrony is introduced. As discussed in previous chapters, synchrony refers to the analysis of a mode of production in terms of a unique theoretical time. That is, a mode of production is not a period in history; it has no beginning and end in real history. Rather, the time of the mode of production is determined by the concepts describing its structure. A diachrony is, in a similar sense, representative of a theoretical time frame. For Balibar, it signifies the time in which the production relations of one mode of production transform the forces of production of another; that is, it is the time of transition.

Finally, I will examine Hindess' and Hirst's critique of Balibar's theory of transition. We see that this criticism is based largely on empiricist epistemological assumptions. However, it signals certain real difficulties in Balibar's concept of the transitional mode of production. These difficulties are examined and corrected in Chapter 8, where I will delineate the concept of the transitional social formation.

Marx employed two approaches to the movements of the elements of a structure in time, both of which have been applied, by various writers, to the problem of transition. The first approach considered is primitive accumulation, in which Marx traces the development of the elements of the capitalist mode of production: free-wage labor and commodity production. Secondly, Marx provided an analysis of the "historical tendency of the capitalist mode of production." The key question is whether the historical tendency implies the supersession of capitalism by a new mode of production. If so, then Marx's analysis of the capitalist mode of production can be assimilated to an essentialist view of history as reflection of the dialectical movement of ideas.

After a discussion of these two approaches, I will discuss Balibar's concept of the transitional mode of production. Finally, the elements of Balibar's diachronic analysis will be introduced.

MODE OF PRODUCTION AS A TRANSITION

Balibar's claim that forms of transition are modes of production is controversial. I will return to this issue in the examination of Hindess' and Hirst's critique, but I will set down here the rationale behind the judgment. The argument appears to be a simple one: since no society can stop producing, i.e., since no society can exist without relations of production, transition between modes of production must constitute particular forms of production relations. That is, they must be modes of production; a mode of production is nothing more than a particular variation of elements that are always present. However, stated in this manner the argument does not follow. The fact that a nation must produce to survive does not imply that periods in which one mode of production is dissolving and another forming must be analyzed as a mode of production distinct from either mode already detailed. On the contrary, as Hindess and Hirst suggest, transition can be studied at the level of social formation (or even at a given conjuncture). To understand Balibar's argument, it is necessary to return to the line of thought presented in Chapter 2. Recall that Balibar's aim is to avoid postulating the suspension of modes of production in an empirical residue of history (which would require thinking of modes of production as models). In order to accomplish this, transitions must be conceived at the same level of analysis as modes of production. That is, forms of transitions must be considered as particular combinations of elements, as a certain type of correspondence between *levels*. Note, however, that a mode of production involves a timeless reproduction of structure, while transition is a transformation of structure.[1] Therefore, the transition from one mode to another cannot consist of the transformation of the structure by its own functioning.

Nevertheless, Marx treats the concept of transition, in some places, as a product of just such an internally caused dissolution: the peasant mode of production dissolves internally, the capitalist mode of production dissolves as the socialization of labor and the concentration of the mode of production "become incompatible with their capitalist integument."[2] This is at variance, of course, with Marx's analysis of primitive accumulation, which is so far from an internal dissolution that it appears as an "enclave of descriptive history in a work of economic theory."[3] As we see below, Marx treats the development of the elements of the capitalist mode of production, in this enclave, in abstraction from the structure of precapitalist modes of production. Whether or not, for example, the growth of merchant capital or the expropriation of the peasantry constitute a dissolution of a precapitalist structure is not investigated. Moreover, a disparity exists between the analysis of primitive accumulation and the analysis of the historical tendency of the capitalist mode of production, a disparity that Balibar sets about to describe with precision.

In classical political economy, the myth of primitive accumulation is a retrospective projection. In this myth, the previous savings of certain members of society enabled them to purchase the means of production to become capitalists. This idea rests on the notion that the formation of capital and its development are part of a single movement subject to common general laws (a myth of an origin homogeneous with a current process, itself misconstrued as an effect of bourgeois legal rights). Marx's treatment of this issue is, first of all, an exposure of this myth and, secondly, a rupture between the history of the formation of capital and the history of capital itself. It poses the problem of the relationship between the prehistory of the capitalist mode of production and the history of an earlier mode of production. However, Marx does not give us a history of this earlier mode of production. Rather, he traces out the geneology of the elements of the capitalist mode of production (free labor; the history of the separation of the producer from the mode of production, and capital; and the history of usury and merchant capital). That is, he analyzes the prehistory of capitalism on the basis of the already known results of this history. Consequently, " . . . the analysis of primitive accumulation does not coincide with the history of the previous modes of production as known from their structures."[4] The transition is conceived in terms of the elements considered as free (free from any precapitalist structure). Marx shows, in this manner, the diversity of the historical roads taken by the elements of the capitalist mode of production, and analyzes certain forms of primitive accumulation (mostly England). While it anticipates the work of later chapters, it might be useful to point out here that bourgeois political economy is still enamored by the myth of primitive accumulation. Its analysis of the transition (bourgeois development theory) continues to project the current operation of capitalism upon its beginnings (upon the transition to capitalism). On the other hand, the treatment of the transition by Dobb, Hilton, et al., rests largely upon Marx's analysis of primitive accumulation.

In addition to primitive accumulation, Marx provides another analysis of capitalist development that touches upon, and has been interpreted as, an analysis of transition: the historical tendency of capitalist accumulation. The difference between these two approaches is that in the analysis of primitive accumulation we are given the elements whose geneology is to be traced but no concept of the structure of the previous mode of production within which this geneology takes place. Recall that the elements of the science of modes of production (laborer, means of production, nonlaborer) *change* with each combination, e.g., the collective laborer of capitalism is different from the artisan—it is a different concept. In the investigation of capitalism's tendency we know the structure of the capitalist mode of production, but we have no knowledge of the elements of the next mode of production. The relevant question is whether the dynamic of capitalism, given by the tendency of the capitalist mode of production, is equivalent to the history of the capitalist mode of production, i.e., does it detail a movement toward the historical future of capitalism. More generally, given that each mode of production has its own contradiction, does the tendency resulting from this contradiction stipulate a future for that mode of production, does it prescribe a specific dissolution? To answer this question, we need to know what sort of tendency and, most important, what sort of contradiction constitutes the dynamic of a mode of production (in this case, the capitalist mode of production).

First of all, the tendencies of the capitalist mode of production are expressed in a variety of movements (concentration of capital, relative overpopulation, and the tendency of the rate of profit to fall), which constitute the development of a contradiction between the socialization of the forces of production and the private character of the relations of production. The specifically capitalist form of this tendency is the contradiction between the increase in the mass of value (and therefore in the mass of profit) produced and the fall in the rate of profit. Of course, this tendency is accomplished by counteracting tendencies, and this can lead to an empiricist interpretation of the law of the tendency of the rate of profit to fall, according to which the law encounters specific empirical limits to its operation. This interpretation lies behind the concept of the law as a long-term trend. However, it is Balibar's contention that the counteracting tendencies are produced by the same movement as the initial tendency.[5] The tendency of the capitalist mode of production is, i.e., a series of contradictory effects of a single cause, and the increase in the mass of profit and the fall in its rate are effects of the increase in the quantity of means of production set in motion by capital.[6] The point is that contradiction is a relation between the effects of the connections upon each other. It is not a logical contradiction (self-contradiction) in capital, and its development does not lead to self-supersession, but to the (cyclical) perpetuation of its conditions. Thus, an Hegelian treatment of transition as a dissolution/succession, in which the internal contradictions of a given mode of production ultimately cause it to self-destruct in such a manner as to create the conditions for the next mode of production, cannot be derived from Marx's analysis of the capitalist mode of production. The internal limits of the capitalist mode of production are limits only with respect to an imaginary development of the forces of production without limits imposed by any social relations of production, and they are but the "limits of each of these connections upon the other."[7] It follows that the contradiction of a mode of production does not develop into a specific dissolution, i.e., that an analysis of the dynamic (or synchrony [see below]) of a mode of production is not simultaneously an analysis of the transition from that mode to another.

Given that neither of the procedures discussed above offer a complete framework for analyzing transition, I will proceed to investigate Balibar's claim that the time of the transition (diachrony) must be set apart and studied in abstraction from certain of the features of the time in which the capitalist mode of production is given (synchrony). It is first necessary to dispel a certain empiricist misconception of the relation between history and dynamics. This misconception locates the dynamics of a mode of production and the transition between modes of production as parts of unique unilinear historical time. Were we to confront the problem of transition while under this misconception, we could tolerate no "differences in principle or method between analyses of the effects of a mode of production and those of the transition."[8]

Marx inverts the theoretical dependence between the concepts of time and of theory; the structures of temporality depend on those of theory. That is to say, the analysis of the relations constituting the structure of a mode of production creates a theoretical time (a synchrony). The effects of the combination of elements are part of this synchrony. The analysis of the combinations of elements in transition makes up a different time, a diachrony, the time "determined by the replacement and transformation of the combination which constitutes the double articulation of the structure of production."[9] These concepts serve, first of all, to describe precisely the difference between the geneology of elements (primitive accumulation) and the development of capital (as a synchrony). Second, the chronological dislocation in the formation of the elements of the capitalist mode of production, suppressed in the dynamic of the capitalist mode of production is brought to the center of analysis. That is to say, the chronological dislocation is suppressed in the sense of being unseen in an analysis of the mechanization of production (the tendency of the capitalist mode of production), in which the dislocation between branches is suppressed as well. In fact, the specific temporality of this synchrony is production in the analysis of this tendency, i.e., the dislocations mentioned above cannot be analyzed in this synchrony.

Finally, what is suppressed by a theory of diachrony? It is precisely the problem of periodization (the portioning out of historical time). This is because periodization necessarily conceives of modes of production against a backdrop of spontaneously given, unilinear time, while a theory of diachrony is centered on the theoretical delineation of a time frame problematic. That is, the determination of the time in which concepts operate is a theoretical task.

I will turn now to the elements of diachronic analysis. The analysis proceeds not element by element but from the point of view of the whole structure. Balibar's particular example of a transition is manufacture, and all that follows here applies to it. As mentioned above, chronological dislocation constitutes the essence of manufacture as a form of transition. Under the real subsumption of labor by capital, the two connections are consistent—the worker does not own the means of production, and the form of the productive forces takes away her/his ability to set the social means of production to work on her/his own, that is, outside of an organized process of cooperation. Under formal subsumption, the laborer's subjection to capital is only determined by her/his absolute nonownership of the means of production, but not at all by the form of the productive forces, which are organized according to craft principles: it seems not impossible that each laborer might return to handicrafts, i.e., s(he) works for capital only because s(he) does not have the means to work on her/his own behalf.

Generalizing from this example, Balibar argues that the form of complexity of a mode of production may be either correspondence or noncorrespondence of the connections; in a homology, the connections are related in a reciprocally limiting way (producing a tendency), but in the case of noncorrespondence the relationship takes the form of the transformation of the one by the effect of the other and the reproduction of this specific complexity is the reproduction of this effect of the one connection on the other.[10] In one case we are dealing with the reciprocal limitation of the action of the two connections, in the other with the transformation of one by the other.

Now the articulation of the levels of the social structure depends on the specific complexity of the articulation of connections. As an example, Balibar suggests that the mode of intervention of science in production is determined by the form of the development of the productive forces in the capitalist mode of production (adaptation of the means of labor to its object). In transitions, the form of law and the state are not articulated with the structure of production but dislocated with respect to it, hence the crucial role of state intervention in the transition. This noncorrespondence between levels is similar to that between connections in that "the mode of intervention of political practice, instead of conserving the limits and producing its effect within their determination, displaces and transforms them."[11]

Thus Balibar attempts to outline a theory of dislocations; such a theory is always constituted by a double reference to the structures of two modes of production. He discusses a precession of ownership in which the property connection precedes and transforms the real appropriation connection, where this latter connection is understood from the concept of a previous mode of production. And he mentions a precession of law in which the legal form of property (along with the state and mode of political intervention) precedes the structure of production, where again this structure is a part of a previous combination of elements.

In conclusion, we have seen that Marx's critique of the retrospective projections of classical political economy led him to produce a geneology of the elements of the capitalist mode of production. Secondly, I have argued that Marx's analysis of capitalism, from which I draw some general principles of transition, does not lend itself to a theory of the supersession of one mode of production by another. Consequently, neither of these approaches offers a complete framework for the analysis of transition. Therefore, I will turn to Balibar's attempt to lay out a theoretical time in which transition takes place. The elements of such a diachronic analysis stem from a double reference to two modes of production and, in addition, are characterized by various dislocations.

CRITIQUE OF HINDESS AND HIRST

In the previous section, I discussed the reasoning behind Balibar's analysis of transitional forms as modes of production. By treating modes of production (including transitional ones) as variations of a universal structure of production, Balibar avoids a crude variety of empiricism, the ideology of models, by which the application of abstract concepts to a given reality is both the goal of theory and an act beyond theory—at its borders, so to speak. According to this view, the problem of transition would be conceived as such an application. Thus, Balibar deliberately suppresses this empiricist problematic by discussing variations in the structure of production (conceived as a double articulation of elements) *in place of* a discussion of history. In this manner, transition becomes a problem, since a mode of production involves a timeless reproduction of structure, while transition is a transformation of structure.

However, the notion of empirical residue has come back to haunt Balibar in the form of the more sophisticated empiricism of Hindess and Hirst. They criticize the project of a general theory of modes of production as (1) essentialist and (2) teleological. By the first criticism they mean that Balibar's project swallows up history, i.e., conceives of the real phenomena of history as expressions of the movement of an essence (the articulation of the forces and the relations of production or the universal hierarchy of functions referred to above). Rather, according to Hindess and Hirst, this structure of production is just a general concept of modes of production, and modes of production are concepts for knowing social formations, and so on through a series of concretizations right up to this morning's *New York Times*. It might at first appear that this debate is better pursued on the more familiar ground of the philosophy of science, i.e., as a debate between realism and positivism. This is not empiricism, according to Hindess and Hirst, since the concrete is not an empirical given but an already theoretical presentation of real conditions.[12] The philosophically trained reader will immediately recognize this as an argument from Kant: an empirical reality must be presupposed but cannot be known since any understanding of it must be inseparably couched in theory. Here, of course, Kant's categories for appropriating the concrete are seductively characterized as class struggle. Moreover, the criticism appears rather harmless, despite the ominous tones in which it is presented, since Hindess' and Hirst's general concept of modes of production turns out to be precisely Balibar's concept of the double articulation of the structure of production. The temptation to let the issue ride on the (probably never forthcoming) answer to the question "do structures exist?" is indeed very great.

However, Hindess' and Hirst's critique of Balibar's essentialism leads directly to their understanding of the meaning of the concepts, mode of production and social formation, and to a critique of Balibar's (and, in fact, Marx's) use of these concepts as teleological. Recalling the discussion of Hindess and Hirst, we know that they wish to replace Althusser's concept of structural causality (causality is the effect of a structure on its elements) with causal relations between events in real history (as opposed to the theoretical history of a mode of production). Let us first briefly summarize Hindess' and Hirst's conceptualization of transition, based on their concept of causality, and then turn to their more detailed critique of Balibar.

A social formation is a social unity of economic, political, and ideological levels.[13] The structure of these levels, i.e., which of them is dominant, is determined by a mode of production that exists if and only if certain conditions of existence are present in a social formation. A mode of production therefore prescribes the limits of variation in the structures of economic, political, and ideological levels; the resulting structure determines a range of possible outcomes of class struggles called a conjuncture. While the economic level of every social formation is structured by some mode of production, the structure of a social formation is not deducible from the concept of its dominant mode of production. Rather, the existence of a particular mode of production (think of the legal conditions of existence implied by the essential role of commodity production in the capitalist mode of production) prescribes limits of variation in the various structures. It follows that the structure of a social formation must be governed by a mode of production, but it may include elements of other modes. These elements, however, may not contradict the conditions of existence of the dominant relations of production.

The presence of a mode is not sufficient to guarantee its conditions of existence; rather, the conditions of existence are secured, modified, or transformed as the outcome of class struggles conducted under the conditions of the social formation. The possible outcomes of class struggles in a social formation are determined by the structure of the economic, political, and ideological levels in the social formation. This structure is referred to as a conjuncture. A transitional conjuncture is one in which the transformation of the dominant relations of production is a possible outcome of class struggle.

The two absolutely essential points are: (1) no general structure of transition is possible and (2) the transition is analyzed in terms of the crucial role of the class struggle in the specific conditions of particular transitional conjunctures.

Note that Hindess and Hirst depart markedly from the concept of a mode of production as employed by Marx. For Marx, a mode of production is constructed of levels. The interaction of the economic, political, and ideological levels defines the unity of the mode of production, and the reproduction of the mode of production depends upon this interaction. For Hindess and Hirst, however, a mode of production is nothing more nor less than the structure of the economic level of a *social formation*. That is, the economic level of society is a structured combination of forces and relations of production, and this structure is referred to as a mode of production. The purpose of this modification is to turn the concept of mode of production into a description (or generalization) of causal relations that are, fundamentally, external to it. The name Hindess and Hirst give to this realm, where everything really happens, is class struggle, but it is very clear that their reading of Marx is empiricist in just the sense discussed in Chapter 2—the object in thought and the real object are opposed, yet connected, and knowledge consists in an understanding of the latter through a grasp of the former.

If no general structure of transition is possible, it is because all of the levels of analysis Hindess and Hirst appear to be juggling (mode of production, social formation, conjuncture, outcomes of class struggle) can be neatly reduced to two: theory and history. But such an empiricist treatment of historicity is characterized by a well-known impasse: either history produces theory, in the sense of presenting a given about which social science can generalize but can never capture, or theory produces history, in which history *is* the working out of some principle, as in the Hegelian philosophy of history. In the former case no general theory of modes of production is conceivable, so the production of such a theory must be a philosophy of history. Hindess and Hirst clearly adopt the former position and see the latter in Balibar. Of course, the claim that a general theory of modes of production is a philosophy of history is standard fare for historicist criticism.[14] While a great many things can be said about the charge that any general theory of modes of production is essentialist, it is first of all urgent to understand that, strictly speaking, any concept of economic determination is a general theory because it posits similarity among different modes of production. This applies as much to Hindess' and Hirst's general concept of a mode of production as to Balibar's structure of production. It is, however, rather a long way from such general notions to a view of history as a predetermined succession of modes of production. Secondly, it is apparent that Hindess' and Hirst's critique of Balibar is an outgrowth of their division of causal analysis into two possible schemas. No middle ground between causality as an outer expression of an essence and causality as relation between external events (external to the structure which explains them) can exist. For them, as for Colletti, social science must choose from the "two main traditions in Western philosophy . . . one that descends from Spinoza and Hegel, and the other Hume and Kant."[15] And, like Colletti, they choose the latter tradition.

However, in their critique of Balibar, which is largely an application of their empiricist understanding of Marx's procedure, they do make an important point. If the causality that governs, say, the capitalist mode of production is internal, and, as we have seen, the tendency of the capitalist mode of production is toward reproduction, then how can transition, if it is to be theorized at the same level of abstraction, be possible? The answer, unfortunately for Balibar's transitional mode of production, is that it cannot. In the following chapter, we outline a concept of transition that is free of this difficulty.

CONCLUSION

I have examined the principal theoretical tools Balibar's theory of transition has afforded us. These include the concept of dislocation, the distinction between a geneology of elements and the tendency of a mode of production, and the concept of diachrony. Each of these will play a role in what follows.

However, we have also discovered a severe limitation in Balibar's transitional mode of production. This limitation involves the impossibility of adequately distinguishing between transitional and nontransitional modes of production.

In the following chapter, I will outline the construction of a transitional social formation, along lines suggested by Bettelheim's work on the transition to socialism—a construction designed to allow us to conceive of the transition without collapsing our analysis into a theory of models.

NOTES

1. Etienne Balibar, "On the Basic Concepts of Historical Materialism," in Althusser and Balibar, *Reading Capital*, trans. Ben Brewster (London: New Left Books, 1977), p. 274.
2. Marx, *Capital*, 1:763.
3. Balibar, p. 275.
4. *Ibid.*, p. 280.
5. Ben Fine and Laurence Harris, *Rereading Capital* (New York: Columbia University Press, 1979), chapter four.
6. Balibar, p. 287.
7. *Ibid.*, p. 292.
8. *Ibid.*, p. 294.
9. *Ibid.*, p. 299.
10. *Ibid.*, p. 304.
11. *Ibid.*, p. 305.
12. Barry Hindess and Paul Hirst, *Pre-Capitalist Modes of Production* (London: Routledge and Kegan Paul, 1975), pp. 2–4.
13. *Ibid.*, p. 12.
14. By "historicism" is meant the view that scientific truth is relative to history, either because history is a product of the development of some idea, or because "real" history provides the test for the truth of a theory.
15. Lucio Colletti, "A Political and Philosophical Interview," *New Left Review*, No. 86 (1978), p. 11.

8

SOCIAL FORMATION AND DISSIMULATION

The subjects of this chapter are the transitional social formation and economic calculation. I will outline the construction of the concept of transitional social formation, adapted from Bettelheim, and its relation to the general concept of dissimulation we have already discussed. In addition, I raise question of the determination of the type of economic calculation characteristic to a mode of production.

In the first section, the transitional social formation is suggested as a solution to problems brought up by Balibar's concept of a transitional mode of production. Specifically, difficulties exist in differentiating transitional from nontransitional modes of production when the transition is analyzed at this level of abstraction. Consequently, the idea of a transitional social formation is designed to permit a more general definition of transition.

The second section introduces dissimulation and economic calculation. The term, *economic calculation*, is meant to capture the form in which surplus labor is pumped out of direct producers in different modes of production. For example, in the capitalist mode of production, surplus labor appears as a quantity of surplus value, and class struggle is over the rate of surplus value and the effects of attempts on the part of capitalists to raise that rate. In the feudal mode of production, on the other hand, surplus labor takes the form of rent, and classes struggle over the forms and levels of rent. In this section, I will relate the concept of economic calculation to the general concept of dissimulation. Finally, after a brief summary of previous results, I will turn to a discussion of the general theory of economic calculation.

THE TRANSITIONAL SOCIAL FORMATION

What follows is an attempt to resolve the difficulties encountered in Balibar's transitional mode of production by elaborating Bettelheim's notion of transitional social formation. I hope to deal adequately with the problem of defining "transitional" and avoid the pitfall of the relapse into a "theory of models."

Balibar concludes his treatise on the analysis of transition with the following remark:

Thus it seems that the dislocation between the connexions and instances in transition periods merely reflects the coexistence of two (or more) modes of production in a single *simultaneity*, and the dominance of one of them over the other. This confirms the fact that the problems of diachrony, too, must be brought within the problematic of a theoretical *syncrony*: the problems of the transition and of the forms of the transition from one mode of production to another are problems of a more general synchrony than that of the mode of production itself, englobing several systems and their relations. . . . The analysis of these relations of domination is outlined by Marx, and it constitutes one of the main fields open for investigation by his successors.[1]

It is in relation to the idea expressed in the passage quoted above that we find the limitations of treating transitions as modes of production. The problem is that modes of production are governed by the dominance of the relations of production, specifically by the effect of those modes of production on the forces of production. A transitional mode of production, as Balibar sees it, is characterized by the displacement of this dominance onto noncorresponding connections: that is, the dominance appears as a transformation of previously feudal forces of production. But this does not adequately differentiate transitional from nontransitional modes of production. First of all, the transition is a guaranteed result since the action of the relations of production is to bring the forces of production into correspondence. Secondly, the laws of motion of the transitional mode of production are determined by the same causal principle as governs the capitalist mode of production. Moreover, the transitional mode of production collapses the transition into a period of capitalist dominance, although this dominance takes the form of a noncorrespondence, that is, of an effect of capitalist relations of production on feudal forces of production. As we shall see below, a similar error involves collapsing the transition into a period of dominance by the feudal mode of production. In either case, the object of the study of transition is lost.

If transitions are to be distinguished from nontransitions, the correspondence of forces and relations of production must be viewed as a requirement for the dominance of a mode of production over elements of other modes. Then, transitions are not inevitable, nor are they reduced to periods within either of the modes of production from or to which they are transitions. However, this requires treating transitions as social formations in which relations from several modes of production coexist, but in which none enjoys the level of correspondence necessary to dominate the others. On the contrary, a transitional social formation is constructed on the basis of nondominance, or a struggle over dominance.

None of the above implies that modes of production or transitions are to be located in "real history," for we do not conceive of the *concretization* of social formation in terms of a juxtaposition of reality to "abstract" theory: rather, it is a theoretically defined complexity, a bringing in of aspects abstracted from the level of mode of production. In this case, the aspects brought into account are precisely the elements of other modes of production. Thus, the concept of transition entails the level of complexity referred to as a social formation, but a transition is only one type of social formation. Consequently, it is possible to treat transitions as social formations without relapsing into empiricism.

We have seen that, in Balibar, the transitional mode of production collapses into a period of capitalist dominance, in which as a specific object of knowledge the transition is lost. To correct this error, we have suggested treating transitions as social formations, characterized by nondominance and by struggle among the classes defined by the coexisting relations of production. However, since the relation of mode of production to social formation is not one of theory to reality, this approach to the transition does not involve "locating" modes of production in the uniform continuum of "real history." In subsequent chapters, the concept of the transitional social formation will be developed in detail.

DISSIMULATION AND ECONOMIC CALCULATION

In this section, the general concept of dissimulation is reviewed, and related to the idea of economic calculation. We see that modes of production may be differentiated according to the form taken by social labor, and the type of economic calculation which, as a result, characterizes the mode of production.

Marx makes it very clear that the type of dissimulation of social relations characteristic of the capitalist mode of production, commodity fetishism, is not a perfectly general concept applicable to all modes of production. Speaking of feudalism, he says,

But for the very reason that personal dependence forms the ground-work of society, there is no necessity for labour and its products to assume a fantastic form different from their reality.[2]

However, it is not difficult to see what general notion of dissimulation lies behind the theory of the commodity fetish. It was not Marx's point, of course, that social relations are transparent to the agents of production themselves under feudalism, but that, looking at feudalism from the point of view of the capitalist mode of production, the fetish is displaced onto noneconomic instances: Catholicism or politics.[3] In fact, in *Pre-Capitalist Economic Formations*, Marx makes the point that the transparence of the relation between the direct producer and his product in noncommodity production is accompanied by the appearance of kinship relations or certain political relations as *natural*, as opposed to being produced by production relations.[4] Moreover, dissimulation applies not exclusively to the economy (except in the capitalist mode of production) but to whatever instance (or level) is dominant in the mode of production.

Balibar wishes to push this idea a bit further by formulating a general concept of dissimulation in the following manner: "Whenever the place of determination is occupied by a single instance, the relationship of the agents will reveal phenomena analogous to fetishism."[5] As example, he describes an analogy between the capitalist mode of production and the Asiatic mode of production. In the latter, the state appears as sole proprietor and as the *source* of "the communal conditions of real appropriation through labor."[6] Such "conditions" include irrigation, a system of communication, etc. Therefore, it appears that the surplus product belongs to and is produced by this higher unity. But Marx describes the same "joining of the function of control or direction, indispensable to the performance of the labour process (the real appropriation of the object of labor) with the function of ownership of the means of production"[7] (property connection) in the section on cooperation in volume one.

Because social labour power costs capital nothing, and because, on the other hand, the wage-labourer himself does not develop it before his labour belongs to capital, it appears as a power with which capital is endowed *by nature*, a productive force that is immanent in capital.[8]

Thus, as we have seen above, dissimulation is a relationship between the relations of production and their legal and ideological forms of expression. The character of this dissimulation, for a given mode of production, is determined by the articulation of the forces and relations of production in that mode of production. The concept of dissimulation is, therefore, a general one.

Bettelheim's development of this general concept of dissimulation brings him to declare that social labor takes different forms in different societies and displays different types of dissimulation. This brings us to the important concept of economic calculation, for the form taken by social labor in a mode of production determines a specific representation of that labor. In capitalism, for example, social labor is represented in the ratios at which commodities are exchanged. Consequently, the specific type of dissimulation exhibited under the capitalist mode of production presents the field of political economy as an homogeneous space (that is, social labor is represented as abstract, undifferentiated labor). This homogeneous space of representation is just the application of the general concept of dissimulation to the capitalist mode of production. The structure of the mode of production is not visible in the forms in which the agents of production view the operation of capitalism. The attempt to understand capitalism solely by reference to the categories presented by capitalism (prices, wages, profits) is the hallmark of classical and post-Jevonian political economy.

By and large, non-Marxist political economy has sought to duplicate the (spontaneously given) homogeneous space of representation in which prices appear in an homogeneous space of another type. Prices are sometimes mapped onto a space of homogeneous labor, as in the Ricardian tradition. In neoclassical price theory, on the other hand, they are represented in terms of utility space. Marx, on the contrary, did not attempt to gaze into the categories of bourgeois political economy in an effort to grasp the essence of capitalism. Rather, he constructed scientific concepts which, by relating the various elements making up the structure of capitalist society, revealed it as an object of knowledge.

As Bettelheim puts the matter, "posing the question of value as a *form* requires the production of the concept of relations of production" and, therefore, of the reconstruction of a structured and complex space.[9] In other words, Marx constructed a (nonhomogeneous) space in which the capitalist mode of production, including the type of economic calculation characteristic of that mode of production, could be situated in relation to other modes of production.

Following Bettelheim, I will presume that, in the analysis of any mode of production, posing the question of the form taken by social labor and the type of dissimulation implied is a necessary step. We have seen above that under capitalism dissimulation is a "joining" of the relations of production in such a way that the surplus product appears to be produced by capital. Under another mode of production, e.g., feudalism, this joining of connections does not occur. While laborers are "separated" from the means of production by the property connection as a result of specific political precondition of feudal rent, the legal/juridical ownership of land, they are not separated by the real appropriation connection, i.e., they retain *some* control over the means of production.[10] Laborers are reunited with the means of production in the form of rent, a relation that takes on a natural appearance.

Once the nature of economic calculation is understood in the capitalist mode of production and in the precapitalist mode of production, the way is cleared for an investigation of the interpenetration of economic calculations in the transitional social formation. To anticipate somewhat, the struggle between the classes defined by the coexisting relations of production in the transitional social formation is located, to a significant degree, in the theoretical region we have marked off by the term *economic calculation*.

CONCLUSION

We have seen that a general concept of dissimulation can be drawn from Marx's analysis of capitalism. Specifically, the instance that plays a predominant role in material production will undergo a distortion analogous to the "commodity fetish" of the capitalist mode of production. This conclusion leads us to a consideration of economic calculation. As seen above, modes of production are characterized by a particular form of dissimulation, determined by the articulation of the forces and relations of production, and by a characteristic type of economic calculation. Capitalism, for example is characterized by an ideological "joining" of the relations and forces of production, and by the expression of social labor in commodity categories.

NOTES

1. Etienne Balibar, "On the Basic Concepts of Historical Materialism," in Althusser and Balibar, *Reading Capital*, trans. Ben Brewster (London: New Left Books, 1977), p. 308.
2. Marx, *Capital*, 1:77.
3. Balibar, p. 218.
4. *Ibid*.
5. *Ibid*.
6. Marx, *Pre-Capitalist Economic Formations*, p. 64.
7. Balibar, p. 219.
8. Marx, *Capital*, 1:333.
9. Charles Bettelheim, *Economic Calculation and Forms of Property* (London: Routledge and Kegan Paul, 1976), p. 52.
10. This formulation is rendered more precise below, where class struggle and the subsumption of the direct producer to the ruling class is discussed (see chapter nine). Briefly, the development of the feudal mode of production implies rendering the tenant a virtual nonpossessor, but the type of development of the forces of production that accomplishes the separation of direct producers from the means of production differs from that of capitalism.

9

THE THEORY OF ECONOMIC CALCULATION

The purpose of this chapter is to lay out a general theory of economic calculation, i.e., one which applies regardless of the mode of production to which it applies.

PREVIOUS RESULTS

In a previous chapter, I examined Balibar's concept of a transitional mode of production. We saw that his insistence that transition be analyzed at this level of abstraction is based upon his critique of a particular misinterpretation of modes of production, that is, as models of reality. Hindess and Hirst claim that such a procedure results in a teleological conception of transition. They rectify the error by introducing an element of indeterminancy into the theory under the title, "class struggle." However, it is difficult not to see in this rectification a smuggling of the empirical residue of real history back into the theory of modes of production. The following remarks are meant to outline a concept of a transitional social formation that neither guarantees any pregiven result nor locates the causal elements of the theory outside of the theory, in either events or in outcomes.

We can think of the relationship between mode of production and social formation in a manner similar to that between production and exchange in Marx's analysis of the capitalist mode of production. Recall that value determines price through a series of mediating forms. Market price fluctuates around a determinate deviation from value—the price of production—where the deviation is determined as the result of the integration of the distribution of surplus value among capitals with the production of value, i.e., as a result of the sphere of production. Now, taking the nature of the determination to be the same for the mode of production/social formation relation as for the relation between values and prices, we can infer that social formations are not the real forms of existence of an abstract mode of production, but, rather, theoretically defined objects, the result of an integration of aspects abstracted from in the course of considering the mode of production. These aspects may be brought into perspective in at least two different ways.

The relation mode of production/social formation may be identified with the base/superstructure relation, as in Hindess and Hirst.[1] In this case, the aspects brought into consideration in a social formation are the conditions of existence of the mode of production, and they are determined within a range set by the mode of production. Of course, the crucial aspect integrated in this case is not class, since classes are defined by production relations, but the theoretical indeterminacy of the outcomes.[2] The concept *social formation* mediates between mode of production (which becomes the economic instance of the social formation) and the conjuncture (a type of social formation, e.g., transitional conjuncture). At the level of social formation, then, the theoretician leaves history to its protagonists, in order to watch the fight from ring side.

It is not the case, however, that analyzing class struggle requires historicism, for the integration of more concrete elements can be accomplished in another fashion. A mode of production may be thought of as a totality of base and superstructure that abstracts specifically from other modes of production. In my view, and this seems little different from that of Bettelheim in *Economic Calculation and Forms of Property*, a social formation consists of an integration of elements of various modes of production and of relations of dominance or nondominance among those elements. Here the problem is to decide the articulation of these elements. Furthermore, in this case class struggle is an aspect of the mode of production as well as of the social formation, but the struggle is more complex in the latter. This does not imply that class struggle is either more or less determined in social formations than in modes of production. Finally, a distinction may be drawn between social formations in which a mode of production is dominant over other modes, that is, where these elements perform functions in the reproduction of the relations of the dominant mode of production or else cease to exist; and social formations in which no mode of production has a level of correspondence sufficient to ensure its dominance.

The latter case is referred to as a transitional social formation and an example is state capitalism (as conceived by Bettelheim) in which the relations and forces of production are capitalist but the superstructural conditions for capital (private ownership of the means of production) have been displaced by the legal conditions of the existence of socialism (state ownership of the means of production and of their products). A mutual limitation (and potential transformation) exists between (capitalist) base and (socialist) superstructure that defines a particular class struggle between workers (through the State) and capitalists (through enterprises).

Balibar's objection to a theory of models is based on a rejection of Weberian sociology from Marxism, as well as of the resultant conception of modes of production as ideal types. The principal effect of such an importation into Marxism would be a guaranteed lack of rigor, since concepts can be brought into the theory, in no matter what order of discourse, so long as they are tagged real, e.g., real events, or real struggles. While this objection would seem to apply to Hindess' and Hirst's concept of social formation, since it reproduces the theory/reality distinction under the rubric, "class struggle," it does not appear to apply to the second concept of social formation outlined above. This is because only objects that are theoretically definable, unlike outcomes, are integrated with concepts analyzed at the level of mode of production. Thus, no attempt is made to locate modes of production in real history.

The upshot of all of this is that while the distinction between mode of production and social formation drawn in my concept of social formation strictly prohibits the analysis of transition as a mode of production, the difficulty is a semantic one only. The reason is that the term *social formation* does not refer to real history, as it appears to for Balibar,[3] and the example of transition on which Balibar places greatest emphasis, manufacture conceived as a dislocation between capitalist relations of production and feudal forces of production, is in my sense explicable as a transitional social formation.

Since Hindess and Hirst hold the laws of motion of a mode of production separate from the outcomes of class struggle, i.e., give to each of them a different status in their epistemology, a social formation can have laws only in so far as it is dominated by a mode of production, and elements of other modes exist only in so far as they do not interfere with the reproduction of the dominant one. Consequently, Balibar's conception of manufacture as a dislocation is rejected; manufacture is treated as a period of feudal dominance in which the dissolution of this mode is a possibility.

In my view, manufacture is the coexistence of elements of two modes of production (feudal and capitalist), neither of which are capable of dominating the social formation. Capitalist relations of production are limited by the existence of feudal relations, as well as by precapitalist forces of production. Such contradictions imply a specific superstructure, i.e., a certain type of degree of state involvement in the economy, and a form of class struggle: a struggle over the effects of absolute surplus value production. The capitalist mode of production is not dominant and, therefore, the elements of the capitalist mode of production as well as elements from other modes of production act not to reproduce the capitalist mode of production but to reproduce the specific relationship between the forces and relations of production that obtains in the transitions.

The transition consists in a transformation of the forces of production (from feudal to capitalist); capitalist production relations cannot develop fully without this transformation, neither can feudal relations be destroyed. However, this transformation cannot be inevitable because that would presuppose a level of correspondence not achieved by capitalism. Such an inevitability would presuppose, in other words, that the transition had already taken place. Consequently, counteracting forces to mechanization are brought into play in addition to a class struggle. Furthermore, the elements of the social formation do not function to reproduce either capitalist or feudal relations (exclusively) but to reproduce the contradiction between the relations and forces of production, that is, to reproduce the transformation of the forces of production as a struggle between mode of production (and between the classes defined by these modes). To put the matter differently, the actions of the classes defined by capitalist relations of production function to establish the (technical and social) conditions for the reproduction of those relations. And likewise, classes defined by feudal relations of production strive to reproduce those relations, but the two actions are (in general) mutually limiting and contradict each other at every turn.[4]

In this manner, Balibar's many useful suggestions concerning the analysis of transition can be preserved while shedding his narrow and constricting conception of the transitional mode of production. Among the most suggestive are the notions of dislocations as characteristic of transitions and the concept of tendency in the synchrony/diachrony distinction.

The nature of the relationship between the forces and relations of production is one upon which all of the transition writers place great emphasis. In all cases, the relations exercise some form of dominance over the forces of production. For Hindess and Hirst, the relations *imply* both a form and a pace of the development of the forces of production. Recall that the forces of production are conceived as a connection between laborers and the means of production and not as the productivity of labor in a purely quantitative sense. Hindess' and Hirst's position might be defensible if one thinks of the double separation of workers from the means of productive forces as well as form of mechanization that renders the worker incapable of setting the means of production in motion. However, in the capitalist mode of production, the relationship between the relations and forces of production is not only logical but *causal*. In other words, the capitalist class is compelled to revolutionize the means of production. The individual capitalist feels this compulsion, with the force of an objective law, as a necessity to lower the cost of production. This is what Balibar has in mind when he refers to the development of the productive forces by the relations of production. However, Balibar also employs this causal connection to define his transitional mode of production as a specific disarticulation of the forces and relations of production, one in which the forces of production are transformed *by* capitalist relations of production. This is where the conflation of levels of abstraction found in Balibar between modes of production and social formation (as I have defined them) takes on serious consequences. For it is precisely this causal efficacy in relation to the forces of production that capitalist relations of production lack in the transitional social formation. And it is this inability that renders the expanded reproduction of capitalist relations problematic. Finally, it is the presence of precapitalist relations of production that limits the transformation of the forces of production and turns the class struggle between capitalists and workers over mechanization into a more complex struggle involving landlords and peasants as well. Briefly then, a dislocation denotes a break in the causal relations between various aspects of a mode of production, and causal relations between aspects of the modes of production constituting the transitional social formation, which is not accessible to a more general or abstract analysis of either mode.

To conclude, the concept of a transitional social formation, here spelled out in more detail, enables me to utilize the several suggestive concepts developed by Balibar in the context of his transitional mode of production, without inheriting the fundamental difficulties associated with that formulation.

In addition, the concept of a transitional social formation casts light on a recent debate over the relative places of modes of production and social formation in Marxist development theory. As part of a general critique of the modes of production approach, Banaji rejects the notion that a social formation can be constituted by several modes of production.[5] On the contrary, the various forms of exploitation are dominated by capitalist laws of motion at the regional and, as we have seen above, the world level.

It is now clear that Banaji's position is an application of the empiricist argumentation of Hindess and Hirst, according to which a mode of production is a general theoretical concept; social formations are historical examples. Therefore, any real social formation can only be described by a single mode of production. Certain production relations may be precapitalist in form, but they are subject to capitalist laws of motion. This leads directly to the concealed wage argument discussed above.

As against this viewpoint, the transitional social formation allows for a class analysis at the point of production without any guaranteed historical outcome. That is, whether precapitalist relations are maintained or destroyed depends both upon the specific strengths of the various branches of capital as well as upon the strength of the resistance of the precapitalist mode of production. The concept is not limited to a fixed and universal relationship between capitalism and survivals of past modes of production. As Wolpe,[6] Meillassoux,[7] de Janvry,[8] and others have argued, under certain conditions precapitalist relations will be maintained in such a way as to provide capital with cheap labor power. Subsistence agriculture lowers the cost of reproduction of the rural labor force, which in turn lowers food prices, with positive effects on the accumulation of capital. Under other conditions, capital transforms agriculture along more classic lines. Of central importance is the determination, at the theoretical level, of the conditions under which precapitalist relations are decomposed, as well as the conditions under which they are recomposed.

TOWARD A GENERAL THEORY OF ECONOMIC CALCULATION

In *Economic Calculations and Forms of Property*, Bettelheim clearly implies that a general theory of economic calculation is possible, a theory, that is, of the forms assumed by the distribution of social labor in different modes of production.[9] A theory of transitional social formations must rely heavily on the concept of economic calculation, for it consists of an articulation of the laws and tendencies of several modes of production, and these laws and tendencies are expressed in economic calculation. It is the burden of this section to show that the principles necessary to derive such a general theory of economic calculation are present in Marx's treatment of economic calculation in the capitalist mode of production, i.e., in the labor theory of value, and thus can be extracted and applied.

First, Marx laid the basis for such a project in his analysis of surplus value as the form taken by surplus labor under capitalism. Marx was concerned that the generality of the concept of surplus labor be understood.

The specific economic form, in which unpaid surplus-labour is pumped out of direct producers, determines the relationship of rulers and ruled, as it goes directly out of production itself and, in turn, reacts upon it as a determining element. Upon this, however, is founded the entire formation of the economic community which grows up out of the production relations themselves, thereby simultaneously its specific political owners of the conditions of production to the direct producers—a relation always naturally corresponding to a definite stage in the development of the methods of labour and thereby its social productivity—which reveals the innermost secret, the hidden basis of the entire social structure, and with it the political form of the relation of sovereignty and dependence, in short, the corresponding specific form of the state.[10]

This is what Balibar is getting at in his description of the relations of production as a connection between the laborer and the means of production: the form in which surplus labor is pumped out of the direct producer is (surplus) value, since it is in this form that the laborer is connected to the means of production, that is, via the circulation of commodities. However, we have seen that this connection really implies a specific type of separation at the direct producer from the means of production, and that this separation is different under different modes of production. In the feudal mode of production, surplus labor takes the form of rent, and, thus, the direct producer is separated from the land by the landlord's legal right of exclusion (as well as by the principal of *nulle terre sans seigneur*), and reunited with the means of production through the payment of rent. However, unlike the worker of the capitalist mode of production, the peasant is not without some control over the labor process, and therefore the two separations are not identical. Yet, neither is it the case that direct producers are separated from the means of production *only* under the rule of capital. Were this the case, then in the feudal mode of production, given a nonseparation of the direct producer from the means of production, the extraction of surplus labor must be accomplished by political means. On the contrary, rent is a production relation, and not an economic manifestation of the political subjugation of one individual by another.

Treating separation/nonseparation as the crucial distinction between feudalism and capitalism has marred certain attempts to understand economic calculation in the feudal mode of production. For example, Kohachiro Takahashi attempts to draw out the analogy between Marx's analysis of value in the capitalist mode of production and economic calculation in other modes of production by beginning with the simplest and most abstract category presented by feudalism and deriving its historical and logical preconditions.[11] This category is the *virgate* (enough land to support one peasant family). Takahashi proceeds, through a series of mediations, to derive the necessity for seigneurial domination on the basis of the nonseparation of the direct producer from the means of production (much as one might derive abstract labor as an historical category presupposed by the exchange of commodities). Seigneurial domination serves as the feudal analogue to abstract labor as a space of representation similar to money. The transition from feudalism to capitalism rests upon the dissolution of these relations of domination, i.e., on the commutation of labor services.

Takahashi's article is a valuable contribution both as a rigorous development of the concept of nonseparation discussed above and as an attempt to understand the categories of feudalism on the basis of Marx's analysis of value. He refers to the various "social existence-forms of labour power."[12] However, Takahashi overdraws the analogy between the space of representation in capitalism and its feudal counterpart. In the capitalist mode of production, precisely because the circulation of commodities play a central role in the reproduction of the social and technical conditions of production, a homogeneous space in which the calculations necessary to this circulation can be made is a requirement of this mode of production. It is just the case, however, that in the feudal mode of production circulation does *not* perform a pivotal function. This is why the space of economic calculation is not necessarily a homogeneous one but is sufficiently defined as a rent relation. A sufficient condition for the separation of the direct producer from the means of production in the form of rent is the landlord's (enforceable) right of exclusion; political servitude is not a condition of the peasant's economic bondage.[13] Consequently, rent can exist in a variety of forms.

The place of circulation in the capitalist mode of production is brilliantly analyzed in *Capital* in the chapter, "Simple Reproduction".[14] It is also in this chapter that Marx's carefully drawn distinction between the relations of production and their forms of representation is most clearly presented. And, as I show below, this distinction is key in Marx's critique of classical political economy. The reproduction of capitalist relations of production, which in combination with the forces of production define a specific (double) separation of direct producers from the means of production, is accomplished by the integration of the process of production with circulation.

It is the process itself that incessantly hurls back the labourer on to the market as a vendor of his labour-power, and that incessantly converts his own product into a means by which another man can purchase him. In reality, the labourer belongs to capital before he has sold himself to capital. His economic bondage is both brought about and concealed by the periodic sale of himself, by his change of masters, and by the oscillations in the market-price of labour-power.[15]

In this passage, Marx analyzes not only the reproduction of the relation of production specific to the capitalist mode of production but the concealment of this relation, as well, in a legal relation, in a juridical sanction of this relation. Once again, the reproduction of capital as a relation of production, one that permits the expanded expropriation of surplus value, requires that labor power circulate in a legal form equivalent to the form taken by products, that is, as a commodity. The wage contract is a legal fiction masking the ownership of the working class by the capitalist class: the reproduction of this ownership requires that an exchange between the capitalists who market wage goods and those that purchase labor power appear as an exchange between an individual capitalist and an individual worker.[16] Wage labor is only a capitalist production relation in so far as it plays the fundamental role in the reproduction of the economic bondage of the laborer to capital, and in this way guarantees the extraction of surplus labor in the form of surplus value.

The distinction between production relations and juridical ones provides the key to Marx's break with classical political economy. Althusser has suggested that a prerequisite for this break was an earlier break with humanism.[17] By humanism is meant a particular critique of civil society (a society of self-interested individuals, i.e., a commodity-producing society) as an alienated expression of human essence. For humanism, and the term applies as much to Jeremy Bentham as to Feuerbach, the truth of such a society (alien human essence) is present in the spontaneously given form of society. For Marx, at least from the writing of *The German Ideology* onward,[18] the given (legal) form of capitalism (civil society) is analyzable only as part of a structure that is not manifested in the way capitalist society appears to its members. The connection of Marx's break with the humanist view of civil society to his critique of classical political economy can be seen in the following manner. Marx showed that the form in which surplus labor is extracted in the capitalist mode of production, the value form, when fully developed, presents certain spontaneous illusions of competition, in which prices are determined as a sum of other monetary magnitudes (the price of land, labor and capital, viewed as returns to factors of production). That is, the field given for investigation by political economy is a homogeneous one. Marx's break was with the object (this homogeneous field) of political economy; it lay in "the construction of concepts that relate to a complex structure, itself articulated at the different levels of the social structure.[19]

The structure of production (a combination of forces and relations to production) implies a distribution of socially necessary labor time among branches of production that meets the social and technical requirements for the reproduction of this structure, and this distribution is effected through the operation of the law of value. The structure of production is not visible in the value form, hence the illusions of competition. In making the distinction between the economic structure of society and the way society is viewed by the subjects who live in it, i.e., between a production relation and a juridical/ideological relation, and by constructing concepts capable of producing the spontaneous subject matter of classical political economy as a form assumed by social labor, Marx opened up the possibility of a general theory of economic calculation.

Within non-Marxist political economy, on the other hand, a general theory of economic calculation is strictly impossible. This is because political economy limits itself to the duplication of the homogeneous space of prices, either in the post-Jevonian world of utility or in the Ricardian world of homogeneous labor. Any knowledge produced in this fashion is relative to the ideology of capitalism which is its foundation. The same may be said for historicist treatments of value theory, e.g., those by followers of Colletti, in which the concepts deduced from the analysis of the exchange of commodities (specifically, abstract labor) are treated as "expressions of the real contradictions of the capitalist mode of production." [20] Here human essence is replaced by capitalist reality, [21] but deriving the concepts appropriate to the analysis of the capitalist mode of production from the spontaneous presentations of commodity renders these concepts historically relative (and relative to an ideology as well).

The generalization of the concept of surplus labor presupposes a concept of labor (which I have called social labor) which is applicable to any mode of production. [22] The form in which the distribution of social labor is effected, and in which, therefore, surplus labor is extracted from direct producers, provides the *differentia specifica* of economic calculation in different modes of production. Once again, the validity of the use of such a concept turns upon the interpretation given to Marx's analytical procedure in *Capital*. Did he analyze value as a form taken by social labor? If so then room exists for differentiating modes of production on this basis. Or, did Marx uncover a rupture between form and essence that is peculiar to capitalist reality, between material production and its social expression? If this bifurcation is peculiar to capitalism, then in other modes of production material production does not assume any form whatsoever, but appears as itself. In this view of the precapitalist relations of production as nondissimulating, just as in the view of precapitalist modes of production as a nonseparation of direct producers from the means of production, a portion of output may be expropriated by political means, but no economic calculation analogous to value calculation in capitalism can be conceived.

In this section, I have argued that a general theory of economic calculation may be extracted from Marx's analysis of economic calculation in the capitalist mode of production. In addition, I have shown that errors in analyzing economic calculation in the feudal mode of productions can result from ignoring the form of separation of direct producers from the means of production particular to that mode of production.

CONCLUSION

In this chapter, I have filled out the concept of the transitional social formation. I have also demonstrated that Marx's critique of the labor theory of value contains the elements necessary to a general theory of economic calculation, upon which the transitional social formation must necessarily rely.

My special interest lies in comprehending the transition to capitalism and, especially, in reviewing the problems of underdevelopment on this conceptual terrain, specifically through an analysis of economic calculation in this context. In reference to the foregoing material, such a transitional social formation involves a struggle between precapitalist and capitalist social relations (and between the classes defined by these relations), and, hence, an articulation of the forms of economic calculation in which relations appear.[23] The analysis of such articulations will require an understanding of economic calculation in both modes of production. Some additional remarks on economic calculation in the feudal mode of production are found below. For the moment, it suffices to mention some of the problems that will be encountered in the articulation of economic calculation in transitional social formations.

Where dislocations occur, either between base and superstructure or between the forces and relations of production, the determination of prices is immediately problematic. Prices in a transitional social formation are, to widely varying degrees, the form in which precapitalist relations appear. For example, Rey treats the irrational price of land as the appearance of a feudal production relation in the capitalist mode of production.[24] More generally, where a dislocation between the forces and relations of production is present, the relation of prices to costs, either in money or labor, is undefined. This leaves certain vagaries in the concept of competition. What is the effect of productivity increases that cannot affect the prices of certain commodities? The determination of wages in a transitional social formation is equally problematic. It is a major tenet of Marx's treatment of the capitalist mode of production that wages are determined in production. While they are by no means determined exogenously in a transitional social formation, they are certainly not determined within the capitalist mode of production.[25] Furthermore, the developed form of the law of value is the establishment of prices of production, but what if the law of value cannot reach this stage of development? What form does competition between capitals over surplus value take in that case?

On the other hand, what is the effect of the expression of the feudal relation, rent, in money? Clearly the relatively simple calculation of surplus and necessary labor times will undergo transformation under this rent form, even if no other change occurs in the relation of production. Economic calculation becomes a site of class struggle. The role of the state in transitional social formations is seen partly in state manipulations of prices. This includes not only the issue of protected markets (a well-known element in the debates over the transition to capitalism in Europe), but also the state's role in the extension of credit.

NOTES

1. Hindess and Hirst, *Pre-Capitalist Modes of Production*, pp. 13–15.

2. It might be noted that, while no theory (as opposed to an ideology) is ever complete in the sense of determining the action of each of its elements, this is never cause to designate any particular theoretical gap as "reality."

3. Balibar, "On the Basic Concepts of Historical Materialism," in Althusser and Balibar, *Reading Capital*, p. 300n.

4. It is Rey's argument that these actions are, under certain circumstances, mutually supportive rather than limiting. I discuss this argument below.

5. J. Banaji, "Modes of Production in a Materialistic Conception of History," *Capital and Class* 3 (Autumn 1977).

6. H. Wolpe, "Capitalism and Cheap Labour Power in South Africa: From Separation to Apartheid," *Economy and Society*, vol. 1, no. 4, 1972.

7. Claude Meillassoux, "From Reproduction to Production: A Marxist Approach to Economic Anthropology," *Economy and Society*, vol. 1, no. 1, 1972.

8. Alain de Janvry, *The Agrarian Question and Reformism in Latin America* (Baltimore: Johns Hopkins, 1981), p. 17.

9. Charles Bettelheim, *Economic Calculation and Forms of Property*, Chapter 1.

10. Marx, *Capital*, 3:791.

11. Kobachiro Takahashi, "A Contribution to the Discussion," in Hilton, pp. 68–69.

12. *Ibid.*, p. 70.

13. Hindess and Hirst, p. 235.

14. See Marx, *Capital*, 1:566–78; Rey, pp. 104–111.

15. Marx, *Capital*, 1:577–78.

16. Rey, *Colonialisme, neo-colonialisme et transition au capitalisme* (Paris: Francois Maspero, 1971), p. 109.

17. See Althusser, *For Marx*, p. 227.

18. K. Marx and F. Engels, *The German Ideology*, (Moscow, 1968).

19. Charles Bettelheim, "Theoretical Comments," in *Unequal Exchange, A Study of the Imperialism of Trade*, by Arghiri Emmanuel (New York: Monthly Review Press, 1972), trans. Brian Pearce, Appendix I, p. 280.

20. See Susan Himmelweit and Simon Mohun, "The Anomalies of Capital," *Capital and Class*, no. 6 (August 1978), p. 72.

21. Lucio Colletti, "Comments on Marx's Theory of Value," *The Subtle Anatomy of Capitalism*, ed. by Jesse Schwartz (Santa Monica, California: Goodyear Publishing Co., 1977), pp. 458–73.

22. Bettelheim refers to this concept as abstract labor, i.e., the labor that reproduces the relations of production, as opposed to the concrete labor of a subject, in order to highlight the distinction between science and ideology (see *Economic Calculations*, p. 37). This invites needless confusion between the generalizable concept of Marx in the earlier chapters of *Capital*. Therefore, we prefer to use the term, social labor, employed by Bettelheim in his critique of Emmanuel.

23. An investigation into transitional social formation involving modes of production other than capitalism or feudalism is beyond the scope of the present

work. The interested reader will consult Pierre-Philippe Rey, *Colonialisme, neo-colonialisme et transition au capitalisme* (Paris: Maspero, 1971); Claude Meillassoux, *Antropologie economique des Gouro de Côte-d'Ivoire* (Paris: Mouton, 1964); E. Terray, *Marxism and Primitive Societies, Two Studies* (New York: Monthly Review Press, 1972); and M. Godelier, *Perspectives in Marxist Anthropology*, trans. by Robert Brain (Cambridge: Cambridge University Press, 1977).

24. Rey, *Les alliances des classes.*
25. Bettelheim, "Theoretical Comments," p. 298.

10

THEORIES OF THE TRANSITION

The leading writers on the subject of the theory of the transition are Dobb, Sweezy, Rey, Brenner, and Hindess and Hirst. Each offers significant insights into transition, but none is in possession of an adequate analytical framework.

We need a concept of transitional social formation sufficiently robust to aid in understanding contemporary problems of underdevelopment, with special emphasis on economic calculation. Consequently, it will be useful to examine several conceptions of the transition from feudalism to capitalism described in the past. These accounts contain the information essential to the construction of an adequate concept of the transitional social formation and, furthermore, since certain paths have already been pursued, they provide a kind of map to this otherwise uncharted terrain.

In what follows, I discuss two errors that appear in analyses of the transition: that deriving a concept of feudalism from Marx's analysis of primitive accumulation, and that of treating the transition as a more or less passive response to events external to the structure of production. The science of society debate over the transition is used to demonstrate the first error. The work of Rey is discussed as a thorough break with the problematic of primitive accumulation, even though he remains a prisoner of the ideology of models in that he always locates transitions under the dominance of one mode or the other. Moreover, his analysis ultimately leads to a different presentation of the commercialization model of Paul Sweezy, according to which the growth of trade preceded and caused the transition. The critique of the commercialization model is strongest in Brenner, and his remarks are applied to Rey. However, he ultimately locates the cause of transition in external events. Hindess' and Hirst's analysis of feudalism is very clear. They avoid seeing the feudal mode of production in terms of a nonseparation of direct producers from the mode of production. However, their treatment of transition is inferior in that they argue that the transition must be analyzed strictly within the feudal mode of production, as opposed to analyzing the transition as a struggle between modes of production.

TWO IMPORTANT ERRORS

The writings on the transition exhibit two significant methodological errors, both of which have been discussed above. The first involves a misapplication of the procedure employed by Marx in his analysis of primitive accumulation. The second is the importation into Marxism of the ideology of models, which treats Marx's concepts as approximations to real history.

As we saw in the opening section, Marx discussed the origins of the elements of the capitalist mode of production in a general way. That is, he discussed them without reference to the economic structures in which these elements were formed. Such a geneology of elements was, by and large, adequate to Marx's purposes, since his analysis was synchronic. His interest lay in differentiating the capitalist mode of production from precapitalist modes of production, and not in analyzing a specific precapitalist mode of production. The results of applying this general procedure, which is a prerequisite for a theory of transition, to the analysis of the feudal mode of production, have produced an inadequate concept of this mode of production. In this conception, the direct producers in the feudal mode of production are not separated from the mode of production. Consequently, exploitation does not take an economic form, but a political one, in which subjects are dominated by other subjects. That this notion is a logical consequence of reducing the problems of the transition to the distinction capitalism/noncapitalism is clear from the following remarks.

In all forms in which the direct labourer remains the "possessor" of the means of production of his own means of subsistence, the property relationship must simultaneously appear as a direct relationship of lordship and servitude, so that the direct producer is not free.[1]

Again, while the effects of this procedure are not felt in Marx's analysis of the capitalist mode of production, they are pronounced for post-Marxian accounts of the transition (as well as for the theory of development, as discussed below). These effects are several: (1) since no economic exploitation occurs (that is, no exploitation based on the separation of direct producers from the mode of production), exploitation must take place through extra economic or forceful means, as in banditry or a state tributary system;[2] (2) no concept of economic calculation, as I have outlined it, can apply to the feudal mode of production; (3) the transition to capitalism is viewed as a liberation of direct producers; and (4) the specific development of the productive forces under capitalism is confused with the suprahistorical concept *productivity* in such a way that the feudal relations of production are viewed as inhibiting productivity rather than developing the forces of production in a determinate manner.

The second difficulty present in most writings on the transition is the Weberian treatment of modes of productions as models. If a mode of production is an approximation to (or generalization from) actual events, then it is these events that cause the transition (or nontransition) from one mode to another. A quest is begun, therefore, for a holy grail that will cause an alteration in the economic structure of society. The object of such a search may be a prime mover external to the mode of production, such as the growth of the market, or an internal indeterminancy, such as the outcomes of class struggle. Considerable theoretical effort must be expended to keep these outcomes, which are never determined by the development of the feudal mode of production itself, from resolving into external factors, e.g., demographic ones, which might explain why here a successful peasant resistance to labor rent occurs and why there a landlord victory results in reenserfment. None of the above should be taken to mean that class struggle is unimportant in the transition to capitalism. We shall see that it is the struggle between relations of production from two modes (and this implies struggle between classes defined by these relations), as well as the interpenetration of economic calculations from both modes, that determines the laws of motion of the transitional mode of production.[3]

However, a second consequence of the ideology of models is the denial of a concept of transitional social formation in which production relations coexist. This arises from the view that, while relations of production imply a certain development of the forces of production (as well as a certain legal structure), these relations do not bring about changes in the forces of production. Thus, for example, the accumulation of value implies mechanization, but this relation of production does not bring about this result either within the capitalist mode of production, or *a fortiori*, in a transitional social formation. It follows that a capitalist relation of production only exists when its conditions of existence are present in a social formation. Thus, the existence of a capitalist relation of production without a capitalist transformation of the forces of production, as in Balibar's conception of manufacture, is impossible. That is, the theory of models involves a modification of Marx's analysis of capital, in which the classes defined by capitalist relations of production act, with the force of objective law, in such a way as to bring about a certain development of the forces of production; this modification is designed to reduce Marxism to a theory of structures only explaining causal relations between events. I have argued above that it is this causal connection that is blocked in the transitional mode of production, and that the source of this blocking is the presence of precapitalist relations of production. The problem with the "one mode at a time" rule is that it forces the theorist to define any corresponding elements as elements belonging to an earlier mode of production. Thus, manufacture is conceived as a period in the feudal mode of production in which certain relations that are apparently capitalist, e.g., wage labor, play a role in feudalism but do not interfere with the reproduction of feudal relations of production. Furthermore, the elements of some mode of production are always in correspondence, and therefore dominate the social formation. The notion of transition resolves to the dissolution of the previous mode of production. This dissolution requires either the operation of some internal contradiction, or outcomes of class struggle that are essentially external, if not to the feudal mode of production, then to the analysis of modes of production itself.

THE SCIENCE AND SOCIETY DEBATE

Having drawn out these two errors, I proceed now to a discussion of certain attempts to analyze the transition, beginning with the Marxist debate over the transition from feudalism to capitalism in Europe. The bulk of the writings contained in the famous Science and Society debate on the transition consists of an all-sided attack by Marxist economic historians on the commercialization model employed by Paul Sweezy in his critique of Maurice Dobb's *Studies in the Development of Capitalism*.[4] The main thrust of the attack lay in a comparative historical reminder that the rise of the market exercised very different effects on different regions of Europe, in places stimulating the expropriation of peasants and the development of three-tiered capitalism in agriculture (as in England) and, in others, bringing about a return to the extraction of rent in the form of labor services previously commuted to rent-in-kind; that is, the spread of commodity production initiated a process of refeudalization. Consequently, the development of capitalism was not sufficiently explained by the growth in exchange relations. In addition, an alternative explanation was detailed along lines suggested by Dobb's original work. Capitalism developed on the impetus of the growth in the market only in those parts of Europe where previous class struggle between landlords and peasants had created an independent, but not freeholding, peasantry. Under these circumstances, commercialization elicited both an expropriation of the landed property of the peasants, from whom rent payments had dwindled to nominal status; and a differentiation of this peasantry into a yeomanry and a dispossessed mass of potential wage laborers.

This peasant victory is sometimes explained as the outcome of class struggle or elsewhere, as due to the influence of demographic factors. In any case, the attempt to discover an explanation in the structure of the feudal mode of production is hardly successful. Peasants respond to rent increases by increasing productivity, either on their own plots, in the case of labor rent, or generally, as in the case of rent-in-kind. But productivity increases are anathema to feudal relations of production because they threaten the landlord's power over the peasant. And, since productivity develops as the productivity of the peasant, it leads necessarily to the liberation of the peasantry.[5]

It is worth demanding a little more precision as to why an increase in productivity liberates the peasantry. There exists a variety of circumstances in which productivity increases benefit the landlord: productivity increases in labor performed on the demesne, and productivity increases in the cases of rent-in-kind or money rent where the landlord can follow them up with increases in rent. More importantly, productivity increases that depend on the landlord's supervision and control of the surplus, such as the use of dikes, mills, large plough teams, etc.,[6] do not lead to an independent peasantry, but rather restrict its development. We know, of course, that rents fixed by custom, a decrease in the extent of demesne land, and the end of labor organized under the supervision of the landlord all occur (in England) during the feudal crisis of the fourteenth and fifteenth centuries. What is not clear is whether all these prerequisites for peasant independence can be understood as effects of the contradiction between feudal production relations and productivity. If not, then the temptation to resort to external explanation, whether to demographic explanation, to commercial catalysis, or to the outcomes of class struggle, is very strong.

PIERRE-PHILLIPE REY

Pierre-Phillipe Rey attacks both of the errors mentioned above. However, while his work is path-breaking, he achieves only limited success, especially in that his break with the ideology of models is only a partial one. Rey, like Dobb, is concerned with the differential effect of commercialization on precapitalist class relations, but he extends this investigation beyond the development of capitalism in Europe to the effect of the market on production relations in parts of the world (notably Africa) that were dominated by precapitalist modes of production other than feudalism.[7] The nature of the opposition, capitalism/precapitalism, is made contingent upon the structure of the precapitalist mode of production. In general, precapitalist modes are resistant to the development of capitalism; but, in the case of feudalism, a relation of mutual interest develops between the landlords and the nascent capitalist ruling class. Capitalist relations of production are able to develop because of the provision of labor power (expropriated peasants) and raw materials (including food products) by the action of the feudal class (actions designed to raise rents). Were it not for the feudal class, direct producers would retain their connection to the land and raw materials would be retained in the natural economy and never become accessible (as commodities) to the urban proletariat. Likewise, the development of capitalism provides a market for agricultural products and thus contributes to the revenue of the landlord class.

This analysis, despite its many weaknesses (discussed below), leads Rey to his most important theoretical contribution: the determination of class struggle in the articulation of two modes of production. That is, class struggle is seen as an effect of an interrelation of two structures of production, and not as a relatively autonomous cause of the evolution of the structure of production.

What leads Rey to this nonempiricist treatment of class struggle in the transition is (1) the differentiation between precapitalist modes of production and (2) the related distinction between a general theory of capitalist articulation (primitive accumulation) and an analysis of the effects of an articulation between the capitalist mode of production and a specific precapitalist mode of production. Thus the differential impact of commercialization on precapitalist modes of production is explained not by the (ultimately exogenous) outcomes of class struggle, but by the class struggle arising from a coexistence of different production relations in a social formation.

This is the basis of Rey's (largely mistaken) critique of Marx's theory of absolute rent. By treating absolute rent as a distribution relation between landlords and capitalists that is the effect of a juridical relation (the existence of landed property) in the capitalist mode of production, Marx bans the class relation between landlords and capitalists from the analysis. Rey goes on to argue that this methodological error will show up as an inconsistency in Marx's treatment of rent. It does not follow, however, that leaving out the requisite elements for a diachronic analysis of a particular issue will vitiate a synchronic analysis of the same issue. Specifically, as we see below, Rey's charge that Marx's analysis implies absolute rents infinitely close to zero is well off the mark. Nevertheless, Rey's suggestions about the place of rent in a transition social formation seem well taken. Rent is a feudal economic calculation; in the transitional social formation, it appears partly as a distribution relation between landlords and capitalists because it is visible in the form of the price of land. That is, it appears in a capitalist juridical form, as a return to a factor of production, and as a form that cannot be reduced to the economic level since such a commodity (land) has no value. However, the relation that exists behind rent is that between landlord and tenant, a feudal production relation.

Although Rey's analysis implies a break with the ideology of models, this break is incomplete. Recall that a feature of this methodology is the impossibility of production relations coexisting in a social formation, i.e., elements of other (nondominant) modes may exist but only in so far as they contribute to the reproduction of the relations of production of the dominant (that is, the only) mode of production in the social formation. Consequently, the object of study is always one mode of production, and transition must be conceived as a dissolution of that mode. Such a dissolution is either determined by an internal contradiction or by outside forces, or both. The problem is that a gap exists between the precapitalist mode of production (or the dominance of the precapitalist mode of production) and the capitalist mode of production (or its dominance). This gap should be the object of any study of transitional social formations, but it is ruled out by the importation of Weberian sociology into Marxism.

While Rey has relations of production articulated with one another, it is always under the dominance of one mode or on another. To say that a mode of production is dominant in a social formation means that the reproduction of that social formation is dominated by the reproduction of the dominant mode.[8] What this somewhat circular definition means is that when, for example, the capitalist mode of production is dominant, other relations of production provide for some need of the capitalist mode of production (such as the provision of labor power) that the capitalist mode of production cannot (yet) provide for itself. Thus, Rey replaces the succession of modes of production with a succession of phases of transition, defined by the dominance of the precapitalist mode of production in phase one, then by the capitalist mode of production in phase two, and finally, in phase three, by independence of the capitalist mode of production.

It is difficult, however, first of all, to imagine how one could tell if a social formation was in phase one or two, since elements of both modes of production exist in each phase. How, for example, can one tell if rent is a distribution of surplus value, or if profit is a distribution of rent? Secondly, it seems that the only choice is between a teleological series of phases and an empiricist determination of the development of precapitalist modes of production by outside forces. In previous chapters, I have introduced a more general definition of the transitional social formation in which the dominance of one mode of production over another is not universally presupposed. The result is an interference in the development of either set of relations of production, a mutual limitation of the effects of these relations on the forces of production and an interpenetration of economic calculations. I will shortly proceed to the development of this concept in depth.

For Rey, the transition is a product of the internal development of the feudal mode of production, but this development is influenced by the growth of the market, in the form of a demand for agricultural commodities. The landlord can get a higher rent by expropriating peasants and collecting rent from capitalist farmers. Note, however, that expropriation will only increase landlord revenues if output increases, and that this requires an increase in productivity (in money terms). Otherwise, the loss in feudal rent will not be compensated for by capitalist ground rent. Of course, if fixed rents have prevailed for a very long time, these rents may be so low that their loss is insignificant. In addition, the increase in productivity in the example on which Rey places most emphasis, the increase in sheep-raising to supply the Flemish wool market, resulted not from any change in technique, as such, but from a switch to an agricultural product that required more land intensive production.

It appears that the convergence of the interests of capitalists and landlords is as much a product of a particular example of transition as is the commercialization model, and in fact its external requirements appear to be the same: destruction of serfdom (beyond repair) and no freeholding.[9] Thus Rey resurrects Sweezy's model of capitalist development by substituting class alliance for ubiquitous economic rationality. Moreover, he treats the history of England as a general case (as opposed to the special cases of France and, presumably, Eastern Europe). I turn next to Brenner, who treats the English case as special, and finds the feudal mode of production, in general, to be resistant to capitalist development.

ROBERT BRENNER

In the discussion of Dobb, I demonstrated how an understanding of feudalism in terms of the opposition, capitalism/precapitalism leads to the identification of productivity, considered suprahistorically, with capitalism. Feudalism is thus incompatible with the development of labor's productivity, and, in fact, this development destroyed the class relations of the feudal mode of production, bringing on its dissolution and the subsequent development of capitalism. However, resort is made to the outcomes of class struggle in order to explain the contradiction between productivity and feudal class relations. Rey, conversely, finds the determination of class struggle in the articulation of two modes of production, but the specific articulation with which he concerns himself[10] amounts to an overgeneralization from a narrow example about the development of capitalism—drawn not from economic life as a whole, but from the feudal mode of production only. As a result, Rey essentially duplicates the commercialization model.

Brenner has acknowledged his debt to Dobb, and his orientation is very similar. However, instead of seeking a contradiction between feudal relations and productivity as such, he maintains that precapitalist relations confine increases in output to the extension of absolute labor.[11] That is to say, class relations in the feudal mode of production imply a certain development of the forces of production. What Brenner has in mind is that feudal relations prohibit the application of machinery to the production process. This limits the ability of agriculture to respond to demand pressure. However, this formulation suggests two interesting lines of development. First of all, mechanization is by no means the only way in which agricultural productivity can be increased; crop rotation, cooperative mills and irrigation projects, variety in fertilizers, and other absolute means are not prohibited by feudal production relations but are, under some circumstances, developed rather rapidly. Nor do they necessarily lead to peasant independence and the dissolution of feudalism; this depends under whose control such development occurs. Secondly, the terms *absolute* and *relative* are borrowed from Marx's analysis of the development of capitalist production: absolute and relative production of surplus value. The application of these ideas to precapitalist development of productive forces suggests an articulation of capitalist and feudal relations in which the type of development implied by feudal class relations is in contradiction with capitalist development. This contradiction places strict limits on the effect of commodity production on the forces of production. I develop both of these suggestions in the following sections.

For Brenner, the first point plays a strategic role in his critique of the commercialization model and the second punctures any attempt to define capitalism as production for exchange. According to Brenner, the commercialization model rests on Adam Smith's concept of specialization. While this term refers formally to the division of tasks in the labor process, the relevant division in Smith's development model is between agriculture and manufacture. For Smith, such a division is limited only by the extent of the market,[12] so that commercialization stimulates the production of agricultural commodities for consumption by urban workers whose labor power develops industry and increases the demand for food from the country. However, as Brenner argues, such a symbiotic town-and-country relationship requires productivity increases in agriculture.[13] Without them, agriculture will be a drag on industry, and rising food prices will raise wages and restrict the development of industry. Such productivity increases require mechanization, according to Brenner, and this type of development is precisely what is prohibited by feudal class relations. Rather, attempts to increase production are limited to absolute surplus labor increases.

For Sweezy, class relations were modified in response to the expansion of trade: lords commuted labor services to money rents in order to render their holdings more efficient. However, in the general case, as Brenner shows, the effect of trade was to cause lords to attempt to increase output by reinstituting labor rents (where they had disappeared) and, moreover, to tighten the exploitation of the peasantry. This was not the case in England, where the ground for capitalist production relations had been laid by class struggle in the fourteenth century: destruction of serfdom and the absence of any development in freeholding. Elsewhere, the rise in trade stunted productivity[14] and took the form of a market for luxuries and military goods. The main point is that, in general, the growth of trade caused a retrogression in the development of the forces of production.

In Rey's version of the commercialization model, the structure of feudalism is such that a rise of a market for agricultural goods will touch off a key convergence of interests for landlords and the nascent bourgeoisie: landed property provides labor power and raw materials as commodities (neither would be for sale if the peasantry owned their land), and the actions of capitalists in developing industry provides a market for agricultural goods, raising money rents. Note the dramatic difference between this view of the articulation of feudalism and the capitalist mode of production and Brenner's. For Brenner, the increase in trade causes landlords to reenserf the peasantry, to overuse the land (underdeveloping agriculture) and, therefore, to limit the degree to which landed property can provide labor power and raw materials.

For Rey, the convergence of interests overwhelms the struggle between landlords and capitalists over distribution (in phase one, with the feudal mode of production dominant this would be a struggle over rent; once the capitalist mode of production is dominant, the struggle would be over the distribution of profits). The faster expropriation occurs, the lower wages will drop, and the more will trade increase and rents rise. That is, the ratio of surplus labor to necessary labor will increase in both modes of production. On the other hand, for Brenner, trade will raise money rents only to the extent that landlords act so as to (ultimately) reduce productivity and reduce expropriations (even reduce commutations). Therefore, any convergence of interest that may exist can only be ephemeral, since reduced expropriations will raise wages, inhibit industry, and lower rents. In other words, the contradiction between relations of production overwhelms the convergence of interests, except where an increase in trade leads to expropriations because (1) reenserfment is impossible, (2) peasants are incapable of resisting expropriations, and (3) expropriations are accompanied by an increase in the productivity of agricultural labor, this latter being due, perhaps, to a change in agricultural product. In the general case, the maintenance of landed property is based not on mutual interest but on the capitalist mode of production's inability to obtain adequate raw materials and labor power from the feudal mode of production.

Brenner's explanation of the special case (capitalist development) rests upon the establishment of favorable class conditions by both (1) the evolution and dissolution of the feudal mode of production and (2) the outcomes of class struggle. It is the project of Hindess and Hirst to rid this approach of teleology by placing all emphasis on the latter source of social change.

HINDESS AND HIRST ON TRANSITION

Hindess' and Hirst's greatest contribution is their thorough break with the concept of feudalism developed by classical political economy.[15] Feudalism is characterized, on this conception, by a nonseparation of direct producers from the means of production. Therefore, the exploitative relation between direct producers and the ruling class is one of political subjugation. Hindess and Hirst argue that, while the relations of production in the feudal mode of production imply a specific political structure, landed property, they are not reducible to politics alone.[16] Rather, direct producers are separated from the means of production through the integration of politics and production, i.e., politics enter into the relations of production in a way they do not in the capitalist mode of production. Nevertheless, an economic exploitation takes place; surplus labor is extracted in the form of rent; the lease agreement reunites the direct producer with the means of production.

As a result of this break, the feudal mode of production no longer appears opposed to the development of productivity as such. Consequently, Hindess and Hirst can describe various conditions under which the development of productivity is consistent with, and in fact implied by, feudal production relations. Specifically, gains in the productivity of labor performed on the demesne are translated directly and entirely into a higher rent rate for the landlord. In the case of rent-in-kind, a fixed proportion of total product goes to the landlord in rent. Thus, the tenant can only increase his/her standard of living by increasing the absolute level of rent. Even in the case of money rent, productivity increases accrue as revenue for the tenant only where rents are fixed.

While Hindess' and Hirst's discussion of feudalism is therefore very strong, they are weak on the transition to capitalism itself. Recall that, for Hindess and Hirst, a social formation is always dominated by one mode of production. Therefore, the development of elements that appear to be capitalist, e.g., wage labor, must be explained on the basis of the feudal mode of production. Instead of contradictions between relations of production within a transitional social formation, contradictions that transform class struggle in that formation, we are given the dissolution of the feudal mode of production. Hindess and Hirst attempt to sidestep the teleology implicit in their argument by the unpredictable outcomes of class struggle, but the idealist character of the argument shines through. A progression of modes of production, in which one mode dissolves in favor of the next (however indeterminate the timing and placement of the dissolution), is nothing but an historical evolution. The modes of production in such a project become a series of negations, and history a reflection of the progress of these modes, a reflection, that is, of a movement of ideas. However, as we saw earlier, Marx broke decisively with the notion of such a connection between ideas and historical reality.[17] Moreover, such a view of history implies a linear concept of time, one in which events take place in pregiven (to theory) temporality. This is opposed to the theoretical construction of a time appropriate to the object of study; in this case, the object is transition and the time is diachronic. Once again, diachronic analysis is founded on a departure from the problematic of periodization.[18] In the transitional social formation, as outlined below, capitalist production relations imply a certain development of the productive forces, and likewise, feudal relations require a certain development of the forces of production. Class struggle, in both modes and in the transitional social formation, takes place essentially over the issue of the real subsumption of the direct producer to the ruling class. However, in the transitional formation, capitalist relations cannot fully develop precisely because they cannot bring about a capitalist development of the productive forces. Nevertheless, the existence of capitalist relations limits and contradicts the development of the productive forces by feudal relations. This conundrum is sometimes explained ideologically as a limitation on capitalist development as a result of immobile labor. However, such a formation, if it is to display its element of truth, must be understood to refer not to legal restrictions on labor's mobility (serfdom) but to an immobility determined by the type of development of the productive forces implied by the existence of feudal production relations, specifically, one in which the direct producer is united with the means of production. That is to say, the means of production function only as an outgrowth of the direct producer's own abilities and (craft) knowledge. Capitalist relations require, on the other hand, that the direct producer be reduced to an interchangeable part, in other words, that s(he) be mobile of a system of social production that is capable of reproducing this reduction on an ever-expanding scale. Each ruling class, in a transitional social formation, strives to extend its control over its exploited class, but the real subsumption of tenants, which as we see below consists of an extension of handicraft production under the control of the landlord class, is in contradiction with mechanization, i.e., with the development of capitalist relations of production.

CONCLUSION

While each of the writers discussed in this section offers insights into the nature of the transition to capitalism, none offers a complete framework for viewing it. I have tried to show the errors in each approach. These errors I have grouped into two types: those based on an (illegitimate) use of Marx's analysis of primitive accumulation and those based on the theory of models, including in this latter group the analysis of transition under the dominance of one mode of production or the other. For reasons given elsewhere, I analyze the transition in terms of a struggle for domination on the part of classes defined by coexisting relations of production. Otherwise, analyses of the transition become analyses of either the feudal or the capitalist mode of production. The transition is thus lost as a theoretical object.

NOTES

1. Marx, *Capital*, 3:790.
2. Hindess and Hirst, *Pre-Capitalist Modes of Production*, pp. 221–33.
3. The main proponent of the ecological theory of transition is, of course, M. M. Postan; see *The Medieval Economy and Society: An Economic History of Britain, 1100–1500* (Berkeley: University of California Press, 1972). Robert Brenner tries to shore up the relatively autonomous nature of the outcomes of class struggle against demographic explanation on an empirical basis in "Agrarian Class Structure and Economic Development in Pre-industrial Europe," *Past and Present*, No. 70 (February 1976), pp. 30–75.
4. Hilton, *The Transition from Feudalism to Capitalism*, pp. 33–56; also see Maurice Dobb, *Studies in the Development of Capitalism* (New York: International Publishers, 1963).
5. Takahashi, in Hilton, *The Transition from Feudalism to Capitalism*, p. 79.
6. Hindess and Hirst, p. 252.
7. The interesting question of the transition to capitalism from plantation systems is studied by G. Beckford, *Persistent Poverty* (New York: Oxford University Press, 1972).
8. Rey, *Les alliances des classes*, p. 165.
9. Rey treats freeholding as a special (French) case in which the secondary contradiction between landlords and capitalists over distribution caused an alliance of capitalists and peasants against landed property. The French Revolution, therefore, destroyed landed property, with negative results for capitalist development that lasted for nearly two centuries; see Rey, *Les alliances des classes*, p. 161.
10. *Les alliances des classes* is principally concerned with the articulation of

the capitalist and feudal modes of production. Rey's work on the articulation of the capitalist mode of production with the lineage mode of production, which we find to be much stronger, is not considered here. See *Colonialisme, neo-colonialisme, et transition au capitalism*.

11. Robert Brenner, "The Origins of Capitalist Development: A Critique of Neo-Smithian Marxism," *New Left Review*, No. 104 (July/August 1977), pp. 25–92.

12. See Adam Smith, *An Inquiry Into the Nature and Causes of The Wealth of Nations*, (New York: Random House, Inc., 1937).

13. Brenner, p. 34.

14. According to Brenner, the labor squeeze resulting from the increase market for grain from Eastern Europe left peasants without enough time even to support the animals needed for fertilization. The resulting soil exhaustion reduced productivity (see Brenner, "The Origins of Capitalist Development," pp. 45–46).

15. While Marx employs this concept as well, the concept's emphasis on feudalism as a barrier to the liberation of the productive forces places it squarely within the tradition of political economy.

16. Hindess and Hirst, pp. 221–23.

17. See Althusser for the similarity between an empiricism that posits such an intimacy between ideas and reality as an expression of the former in the latter (absolute idealism), and one which posits the connection as a grasping of the truth of reality in theory (epistemological idealism); see Althusser, "The Object of *Capital*," in Althusser and Balibar, pp. 188–93.

18. Balibar, in Althusser and Balibar, *Reading Capital*, p. 286.

11

ECONOMIC CALCULATION IN THE CAPITALIST AND FEUDAL MODES OF PRODUCTION

In this chapter, I look at the way in which class struggle is reflected in economic calculation in, first, capitalism and, second, the feudal mode of production. Of key interest, in the former, is the designification of prices that occurs as a result of the development of the capitalist mode of production.

We see that, in both modes, class struggle takes place over the control of the production process. In the capitalist mode of production, the control is placed in the hands of the capitalist class by the form of the development of the forces of production. In the feudal mode of production, such real subsumption requires that the individual landlord engage directly in the control of the production process. I argue that feudal relations of production determine a specific (decentralized) development of the forces of production.

THE CAPITALIST MODE OF PRODUCTION

Before discussing economic calculation in feudalism, it will help to recall Marx's analysis of economic calculation and class struggle in the capitalist mode of production. Surplus labor, in capitalism, takes the form of surplus value. Differentiating between capital in general, a relation between classes, and competition among individual capitals, Marx notes that the survival of capital depends on raising the rate of surplus value. This is accomplished both by increasing the duration and/or the intensity of labor (increasing surplus labor time) and by raising the productivity of the labor that produces, directly and indirectly, the commodities necessary to the reproduction of labor power (reducing necessary labor time).

This relation between classes, however, is not immediately visible. On the contrary, class struggle in the capitalist mode of production appears as competition among individual capitals, a competition that occurs through the minimization of costs. That is, class struggle takes the form of a determination of wages, profits and relative prices. Note that competition among capitals is not a voluntary process but results when individual producers feel the coercive effect of the law of value: a tendency exists to lower the unit value of each commodity, i.e., to expend only the amount of labor time considered socially necessary. This mechanism, i.e., this theoretical space of socially necessary labor time, distributes labor expenditures in such a way as to provide the technical and social requirements for the reproduction of the agents of production as classes. The process brings the worker back to the factory gates as a seller of labor power and, also brings her/his product to those same gates to purchase that labor power.

The form in which the ratio of surplus labor to necessary labor is increased in the capitalist mode of production brings about a particular development of the forces of production, one in which the laborer is increasingly stripped of any connection to the labor process, except for her/his connection via capital. That is to say, not only is the individual laborer a nonowner of the means of production, but the form of development of the productive forces (mechanization) renders her/him incapable of putting the means of production into operation. It is only in this latter case that labor power is fully separated from the laborer, that the laborer is rendered an interchangeable part, and that the value form is fully developed. Thus, the form in which the relations of production are expressed, the economic calculation, implies a certain transformation of the forces of production, and cannot develop without this transformation.

However, at the same time that such a correspondence is required for the development of the value form, so does this transformation of the productive forces intensify the contradiction between value and use value, between the relations and forces of production. Putting the matter most generally, the more fixed capital is applied to production, the less does the law of value provide the material and social conditions for the expanded reproduction of capitalist production relations. The modern writer who has most discussed the designification of prices in the capitalist mode of production is Bettelheim. Bettelheim is in complete concordance with Balibar's formulation of the form of the productive forces corresponding to capitalist property as a unity of the means of labor and the object of labor, or rather, an unceasing adaptation of the means of labor to the object (the machine head, for example). Thus the transition to socialism inherits techniques of production that are capitalist. The growth in the technical composition of capital and the apparently necessary growth in the size of the units of production in order to obtain a reduction in costs are effects of the capitalist property relation, specifically (Bettelheim adds) effects of the laws of centralization and concentration of capital. Bettelheim returns several times to the concept of the *socialization* of labor, but the theme is always the same. This theme is the loss of meaning to which prices are subjected as a result of the socialization of labor. The result of this is a political intervention in the determination of prices. Note that Bettelheim is expressly discussing the real appropriation connection. As large industry develops, the creation of use-values depends less on direct labor time and more on those "agencies set in motion during labor time, whose powerful effectiveness is itself in turn out of all proportion to the direct labor time spent on their production, but depends rather on the general state of science and on the progress of technology."[1] That is, the fact that products of particular activities have overall social effects (education, scientific research, public health, and even branches of production whose development profoundly modifies the general conditions of production, e.g., transport, electricity) consequently means that the price at which the products of these activities can be sold on the market is deprived of meaning. In the capitalist mode of production, at "a particular level of socialization of the productive forces the price mechanism can no longer function for a part of capitalist production; hence, there develops nonprofitable production, political subsidization, and the recourse to monetary calculation, resulting in the intervention of prices other than market prices."[2]

To the extent that labor is socialized, the price system will serve less and less as a system of accounting in the sense of welfare economics. This intensification of the contradiction between use-value and value (between the real appropriation and property connections) results from the increasing adaptation of the means of labor to the object of labor (that is, the development of large-scale industry) and from the corresponding naturalness of production, i.e., its reliance on science and on intersectoral connections of every sort.

The result is that the distribution of labor expenditures determined by the law of value is inadequate to the expanded reproduction of capital. This fact is relevant to development theory, especially to a development strategy based on the importation of techniques from advanced capitalist social formations. Furthermore, it explains the necessity of political intervention in the price system in advanced capitalism.

As Marx puts the matter,

As soon as labour in the direct form has ceased to be the great well-spring of wealth, labour time ceases and must cease to be its measure, and hence exchange value (must cease to be the measure) of use value. . . . Capital itself is the moving contradiction, (in) that it presses to reduce labour time to a minimum while it posits labour time, on the other side, as sole measure and source of wealth.[3]

This is how Marx treats the contradiction in the *Grundrisse*. In *Capital*, the effect of the transformation of the forces of production becomes the law of the tendency of the rate of profit to fall. Here, the form of development of the productive forces (rising technical composition of capital) undercuts the profitability of production. Thus the designification of the value form provides a theoretical space in which the specific rhythm of capitalist crisis and accumulation can be studied as a theoretical object.

In sum, class struggle in the capitalist mode of production takes place over the subsumption of labor to capital, and this, we have seen, involves the transformation of the forces of production. Secondly, the specific dynamic of the capitalist mode of production is comprehended in terms of the effect of the type of development of the productive forces particular to capitalism on the relation between capitalist economic calculation and the distribution of social labor.

THE FEUDAL MODE OF PRODUCTION

Clearly, a prerequisite for any theory of economic calculation in feudalism is a break with the conception of the feudal mode of production based on the opposition, capitalism/noncapitalism, for we hve seen that such a conception reduces exploitation to a political relation between subjects. On the contrary, feudalism is characterized by an integration of politics and production, in which the feudal production relations are no more reducible to their political conditions of existence than are capitalist relations reducible to commodity production. The formal subsumption of the direct producer (the tenant) to the ruling class (the landlord), the formal separation, that is, of the direct producer from the means of production, is accomplished by landed property. The tenant is separated from the means of production (as a non-property holder) by the landlord's right of exclusion. S(he) is reunited with the land in the rent form. The real subsumption of the tenant to the landlord involves the direct control over production by the landlord.

It is wrong to suppose that economic coercion is particular to capitalism, that, in other words, there is no distribution of labor expenditures into more productive channels in the feudal mode of production.[4] What can be said, of course, is that coercion based on socially necessary labor time implies the capitalist mode of production. A different theoretical space for economic calculation exists in the feudal mode of production, and the coercion of producers takes place in a different form. The landlord must maintain control over the surplus—this is the economic basis of his power. But this surplus appears as a deduction from total product and not as a quantity of labor time. Consequently, the peasant has a general interest in the productivity of labor, although conditions can arise in which s(he) will wish to suppress the development of the productive forces. The peasant is constrained to produce a surplus by the double bind: (1) the landlord's right of exclusion and (2) the principle *nulle terre sans seigneur* (no free land). Thus, socially necessary labor is expressed not in time, but in product, and the social necessity refers to production at a rate necessary to reproduce feudal class relations, i.e., the reproduction of the tenant as a nonowner, in confrontation with the landlord as owner in control of the surplus product.

I turn below to a consideration of the specific form of development of the productive forces implied by feudal production relations. An understanding of a mode of production will not be scientific if it is based on a transhistorical concept of the development of the productive forces. In this context, Brenner's concept of absolute surplus labor extension, while it rules out mechanization, is not adequate to the description of the type of development of the productive forces in the feudal mode of production. Increases and the duration and intensity of labor will have little effect on output, precisely because productivity is so low. At a minimum, a concept of the forces of production in feudalism must allow for increasing productivity through changes in the use of land, new animals, irrigation and drainage projects, and crop rotation.

The feudal mode of production implies a specific transformation of the productive forces. Class struggle takes place over the subsumption of the tenant to the landlord. This struggle involves the various forms that rent takes. The landlord strives for direct control over the production process. This is most easily accomplished under a system of labor rent. For here, the landlord is the agent of coordination for a variety of production activities. The ratio of necessary to surplus product is determined as a function of the ratio of rented to demesne land and of the duration of the labor performed on the demesne. In addition, the landlord can exercise control over the conditions of production on rented land through her/his control over the size of the units of tenure, e.g., the unit of tenancy may be smaller than the unit of production, in which cooperation, under the supervision of the landlord is required. Finally, the landlord controls surplus product; only s(he) can enable the construction of mills, drainage works, and irrigation projects that extend beyond the limits of the unit of individual tenancy.[5] Whether or not the tenant can lower the rate of exploitation by increasing the productiveness of her/his labor depends on the degree to which the landlord has direct control over the production process. For example, an increase in productivity on rented land will lower the rate of exploitation if an only if the ratio of rented to demesne land does not fall as a result. Likewise, a peasant can raise her/his standard of living by increasing productivity where surplus labor is extracted in the form of rent-in-kind, but only if rent is a fixed proportion of total output. More generally, the productiveness of peasant labor is a threat to the landlord in inverse proportion to the extent of her/his control over the production process.

Control over production by the landlord is least direct in the case of money rent. Under conditions of money rent, the ratio of surplus to necessary labor comes under the influence of another form of economic calculation, and of events occurring in distant parts of the world. Because money rent implies commodity production, it represents the introduction of circulation into feudal class relations, relations which are therefore rendered less direct. However, it is not the case that money rent necessarily leads to an independent peasantry. On the contrary, as Hindess and Hirst point out,[6] market conditions can produce a shortfall in rent, and lead to the piling up of debt on the part of the tenant, debt that may be paid in labor services.

In considering the effects of commodity production in the feudal mode of production specifically, the role of money rent and wage labor, it is vital to keep the synchrony/diachrony distinction in mind. In so far as interest lies in the capitalist mode of production, as opposed to the articulation of feudalism with capitalism, i.e., in so far as concern is over a synchronic analysis of economic calculation, then commodity categories may be treated along lines suggested by Marx's analysis of capitalist ground rent.[7] There, rent appears as a distribution of surplus value, and thus, as an economic effect of a juridical relation. Landed property is a relation between capitalists and landlords, where the latter are not a class, properly speaking, but rather make up a fraction of the ruling class. Clearly, in a diachrony, the same element would be treated as a relation of production, a class relation between landlords and tenants articulated with capitalist relations and, therefore, having an expression in capitalist economic calculations, as a price. However, as we see below, no logical inconsistency appears in a synchronic treatment of rent as a distribution relation in the capitalist mode of production.

Similarly, the treatment of wage labor in a synchronic analysis of the feudal mode of production must show it to be a distribution relation between landlords and tenants who employ wage labor in order to pay rent. Diachronically, on the other hand, wage labor will appear as a capitalist production relation, one that exercises a weakening effect on the rent relation in which it is expressed. Moreover, a synchronic treatment of commodity categories cannot be extended acritically into an analysis of the transitional social formation; otherwise, such an analysis reduces to a theory of the dissolution of the feudal mode of production, a dissolution affected either by the workings of an internal contradiction or, as for Hindess and Hirst, by class struggle. Since they have (correctly) left behind the ubiquitous contraction between productivity and property, yet do not offer a diachronic analysis, the transition cannot be defined for them as a theoretical object. It can only be defined without rigor, as a period in which the dissolution of the feudal mode of production is a possible result of class struggle,[8] i.e., a period of transition is one in which transition is possible.

I have discussed class struggle and economic calculation in the feudal mode of production and the treatment of commodity categories, including a digression on Marx's treatment of capitalist ground rent. What remains is the specific relation of the forces of production to property in the feudal mode of production. What type of development is implied by feudal relations of production, i.e., by the extraction of surplus labor in the form of rent and by the integration of production and politics (in the form of landed property)? Once again, the answer to this question cannot be found in a conception of feudalism that reduces it to a mirror image of the capitalist mode of production in terms of the opposition, productivity/nonproductivity.

We have seen, first of all, that Brenner's concept of absolute labor is not adequate to the task I have set. It is a concept borrowed from Marx's analysis of the development of the capitalist mode of production (one which, as we see below, is crucial in the analysis of the transitional social formation) and applied retrospectively to precapitalist relations on the forces of production. More importantly, it identifies productivity increases with capitalist productivity increases (through mechanization).

What must be reproduced in the rent form is (a) a sufficient surplus product for the physical maintenance of the ruling class, and (b) the specific subsumption of the direct producer (the reproduction of the laborer and nonlaborer as tenant and landlord). For the latter, the tenant must be reproduced as a nonowner. This much is very clear. From this point of analysis, two directions are possible. One, the reproduction of the tenant as a nonowner must be accompanied in such a manner that s(he) remain a possessor of the means of production. This is the approach favored by Hindess and Hirst, and they add that were the landlord to try to alter the methods of production implied by independent peasant production on demesne land, s(he) would incur prohibitive supervision and instruction costs. This argument seems very weak. First of all, it is precisely such direct control over production that will allow the subsumption of the direct producer in the feudal mode of production, as we have seen above. Secondly, feudal property relations do not imply any degree of control over production by the tenant, but only a compulsion on her/his part to produce surplus product. In fact, the reproduction of the tenant as a nonowner would seem to imply a development of the forces of production that gives possession to the landlord, since if the tenant retains possession s(he) can conceivably increase her/his productivity (within limits set by the unit of tenancy) to the point of effective ownership, i.e., nominal rent. Moreover, the argument depends on the appearance of a tendency in the feudal mode of production to maintain independent peasant production (despite countertendencies), but the maintenance of independent peasant production is no more a tendency in the feudal mode of production than is the maintenance of artisan production in the capitalist mode of production.

All of the above suggests the following alternative formulation. In order that the specific subsumption of the tenant be reproduced, the tenant must be reproduced as a nonowner and, in the most developed forms of the feudal mode of production, as a virtual nonpossessor as well. The specific forms of the development of the productive forces is given by the integration of politics into production, which determines a highly decentralized form of development. Recall that formal subsumption involves (1) the enforcement of the right of exclusion and (2) no free land. Together, these require the parcelling out of land among relatively autonomous landlords. Thus, fedual class relations are antagonistic not only to the capitalist form of centralization of the means of production (mechanization), but to any connection between units of production, such as commodity production, or connections between agricultural production units via a worker's state, as in the experiments that took place in this direction during the Cultural Revolution in the People's Republic.

While decentralized production includes division of labor along handicraft lines, it excludes the division of the process or production itself in the form of a piling up of dead labor, for this requires specialized and nonautonomous production units. For the same reason, while it includes a variety of improvements in agricultural technique, it precludes the full separation of agriculture and industry, i.e., the division of the production process into departments. Finally, feudal relations imply a development of the forces of production that precludes a *capitalist* separation of the direct producer from the means of production—in precluding mechanization they also rule out the capitalist form of the real subsumption of the direct producer to capital. This limit on the development of the productive forces is often described as an immobility of labor, or as feudal monopoly. As we see below, within the transitional social formation, these elements appear as barriers to the establishment, that is, of the theoretical space for such calculation: socially necessary labor time. The main point, however, is that such monopoly or immobile labor does not result from legal restrictions on the movement of factors. The existence of such legal restrictions are, rather, conditioned upon a certain development of the forces of production, one different from the reduction of the laborer to an interchangeable part, and based on production relations that cannot survive this reduction.

CONCLUSION

I have argued that classes, in both the capitalist and feudal modes of production, struggle over control of the production process. However, in the case of the feudal mode of production, this struggle is much more direct. In the capitalist mode of production, workers struggle over the effects of real subsumption, whereas in the feudal mode of production, landlords and tenants struggle directly for control over production. A second difference is that, in the capitalist mode of production, the relations of production imply an increasing centralization of the forces of production, leading to what I have termed the designification of prices. In the feudal mode of production, the development of the forces of production is, necessarily, decentralized. Therefore, while feudal economic calculation suffers a certain designification in the transitional social formation (see the next section), this designification is not a result of the specific transformation of the forces of production characteristic of the feudal mode of production.

NOTES

1. Marx, *Grundrisse, Foundations of the Critique of Political Economy*, (New York: Vintage Books, 1973), pp. 704–5.
2. Bettelheim, *Economic Calculation*, p. 42.
3. Marx, *Grundrisse*, pp. 705–6.
4. Brenner, "The Origins of Capitalist Development," p. 30.
5. Hindess and Hirst, *Pre-Capitalist Modes of Production*, p. 253.
6. *Ibid.*, p. 247.
7. Marx, *Capital*, 3:748–72.
8. Hindess and Hirst, p. 278.

12

THE THEORY OF ECONOMIC DEVELOPMENT REVISITED

In this chapter, I develop the analysis of the transitional social formation. At this level of analysis, as mentioned above, no particular relations of dominance are implied. In the transitional social formation, the determination of prices by labor time is only partial. This exercises a series of effects that are analyzed below. Furthermore, feudal economic calculation is affected by the existence of capitalist relations of production. Most importantly, it is argued that the contradiction between relations of production is more general than the sort of class alliance discussed by Rey.

THE CONCEPT OF THE TRANSITIONAL SOCIAL FORMATION

The object to be defined in this section, the transitional social formation, must be distinguished from conceptions of transition based upon the dominance of one mode of production over elements of others in a social formation. That is, I wish to deal with social formations in which no mode of production enjoys a level of correspondence that will guarantee its domination of the social formation, rendering the existence of elements of other modes contingent upon the reproduction of the dominant mode. As a result, I am less interested in the discovery of a catalyst that would move society from the domination of feudalism to the dominance of the capitalist mode of production (the growth of the market, for example) than in the analysis of the effects produced in capitalist (feudal) economic calculations as a result of the existence of feudal (capitalist) relations of production in the transitional social formation. For example, money rent will appear both as an irrational price (irrational in the sense that the price of labor or of money is irrational) and as a devolved rent form undetermined by the distribution of social labor necessary to the reproduction of feudal relations of production. Behind the economic calculation—money rent—lies not one but two class relations, one between capital and labor and the other between landlord and tenant.

One resolution of the transitional social formation may be a restoration of feudalism, at least in some sectors. In that case, elements of capital will serve to reinforce feudal relations, to "double these relations ideologically."[1] Another result can be the transition of capitalism, which will render rent a survival that only exists in so far as it aids in the reproduction of capital. Study of these modes is a necessary but not sufficient condition for the study of transition. Furthermore, no time limit exists on the transitional social formation, since, as we saw in the opening section, the chronology of modes of production (periodization) is suppressed in diachronic analysis in favor of chronological dislocation within the transitional social formation, between base and superstructure as well as between the forces and relations of production. It should also be noted that nothing in the transitional social formation, as conceived here, precludes a socialist resolution of this transition, although the conditions for such a development are uniformly abstracted from in what follows.

As we saw in the previous section, while the presence of commodity categories does not necessarily show up as an inconsistency in the synchronic analysis of the feudal mode of production, attempts to extend this synchronic analysis into the study of transition will necessarily be onesided. As an example, Hindess and Hirst try to understand the determination of wages and prices in the period of manufacture purely in terms of the operation of the feudal economy.[2] Thus, labor is supplied by expropriations of peasants, and the productivity of the remaining tenants determines the demand for labor through its effect on wages, and, therefore, on profits. However, even if wages were entirely determined in the feudal sector, i.e., even if every subsistence good were produced in that sector alone, the profit level would depend upon the quantity of surplus labor time performed, labor time over and above that necessary to purchase wage goods. The latter is determined in struggles between capitalists and wage laborers, not in the feudal mode of production, and it affects the expansion of capitalist relations and consequently the demand for agricultural products and the level of rent in the precapitalist sector.

I have discussed manufacture as a dislocation between the forces and relations of production, one in which the effect of capitalist production relations on the forces of production is blocked by the existence of pre-capitalist relations. However, in order to understand the significance of commodity categories in the transitional social formation, the wage-labor relation as a legal relation must be distinguished from wage labor as a class relation. As a legal relation, that is, an an implication of capital as a relation of production, wage labor simply refers to the existence of wage contracts, the legal freedom of the worker to choose among employers. As a production relation, wage labor implies the expanded extraction of surplus labor in the form of surplus value, the integration of circulation and production and the representation of labor power in the space of socially necessary labor time (the value of labor power). The transitional social formation conceives of wage labor as dislocated in this sense, i.e., in the sense of a noncorrespondence between base and superstructure. In such a dislocation, (1) workers are able to produce their own subsistence without always selling their labor power (e.g., the day-laborer who also maintains a food-producing plot), (2) workers are not fully separated from control of the labor process (the labor process is of the handicraft type in which the development of industry depends crucially on the development of the labor force and its craft skills) and (3) wage goods are produced outside of the capitalist mode of production, so that prices are determined, at least in part, by noncapitalist production relations. Of course, just as the presence of feudal relations determines a disarticulation within capitalist relations, so does the presence of capitalist production relations result in dislocated feudal relations. This is seen in money rent, in which the form of rent presents systematic barriers to the direct control over production by the landlord.

The consideration of the development of the value form in the transitional social formation places us on the terrain marked out by the debate over the "historical transformation problem."[3] It is by no means my intention to review this debate, except to note that its central question, whether the determination of price by value varies over the course of the development of capitalism, cannot be answered in an adequate manner in a purely synchronic treatment of the capitalist mode of production. What a diachronic analysis of the problem indicates is that the content of the value form, in the transitional social formation, is different from this content in the capitalist mode of production, and that this is due to the dislocation between capitalist relations of production and the forces of production. Once again, prices are determined by socially necessary labor time only to the extent that capitalist relations dominate other relations of production. So long as this dominance is a point of struggle, as in the transitional social formation, labor time has only a partial influence on prices. Consequently, prices of production are not formed in the transitional social formation. As Marx puts the matter,

And it is competition of capitals in different spheres, which first brings out the price of production equalizing the rates of profit in the different spheres. The latter process requires a higher development of the capitalist mode of production than the previous one.[4]

What precludes the formation of production prices, and therefore, the development of the theoretical space of socially necessary labor time, is the effect of feudal production relations on capitalist development of the forces of production. Such an effect is referred to as feudal monopoly, and it determines a distribution of surplus value toward the least productive spheres. Feudal monopoly price is the result of superprofits in sectors into which the mobility of labor (hence of capital) is inhibited by the need for craft skills.[5]

The limitations placed upon capitalist development of the productive forces by such a distribution are obvious. What happens, however, if despite these limitations a capitalist introduces labor-saving devices to lower the cost of production? Surplus value within the sector in which the innovating capitalist operates is temporarily distributed toward the most efficient production, and the increase in the technical composition of capital and the rise in the rate of surplus value generate the dynamic described by Marx's law of the tendency of the rate of profit to fall. Two points should be noted about how this tendency exercises effects in the transitional social formation. First of all, the dynamic of capitalism presupposes the determination of the price of labor by the value of labor power. In the transitional social formation, the wage is determined in part by precapitalist social relations. Consequently, while mechanization may adversely affect the overall profitability of capital, limits are placed on its ability to raise the rate of surplus value. Moreover, the tendency to produce luxury or military goods for the market will inhibit the cheapening of the elements of constant capital, thus subverting another counteracting cause to the tendency of the rate of profit to fall. Secondly, however, I have already remarked upon the existence of barriers to the formation of a general rate of profit. Thus, the (negative) effects of mechanization on profitability are concentrated in the most mechanized sectors.

Under such conditions, capital is restricted to increasing the rate of surplus value by absolute means. Furthermore, because the expansion of capitalist relations is inhibited, the expropriation of the peasantry is no guarantee that propertyless peasants will become wage laborers. On the contrary, there is a strong tendency toward the decomposition of wage labor, as a result of which marginalized individuals seek subsistence in a variety of ways.

The above tendencies and contradictions are expressed in the partial replacement of feudal economic calculation. Full replacement would require the full development of the capitalist mode of production and the correspondence of the relations and forces production, which would guarantee production at a rate socially necessary to the reproduction of capitalist relations. Partial replacement is characterized by the predominance of categories like feudal monopoly price and money rent.

Money rent is a barrier to the development of capitalist relations; it is described by Marx as a deduction from surplus value, and as such it fetters capitalist development of the forces of production. It is just as true, however, that profit is a deduction from rent, and one that restricts the control of the landlord over surplus product. Consequently, money rent is a designified rent form, the maximization of which does not ensure the reproduction of feudal production relations. Under such a designification of the rent form, rents come to depend on international trade, and the landlord class requires the protection of the state (in a form very different from the guarantee of the right to exclude tenants). At the same time, capitalist production requires state intervention in the form of protected industries. Therefore, the conflict between modes of production is fought out, to some extent, in the state.[6]

The most important point is that the intrinsic contradiction (between feudal and capitalist relations) of the transitional social formation is more general than the class alliance discussed by Rey. Such an alliance, between capitalists and landlords, is the result of a special case in which the distinction between feudal and capitalist development is rendered irrelevant by the switch from corn to wool production, which required less labor. In the more general case, the effect of the market is to retard both capitalist and feudal development of the productive forces. Where agricultural productivity is inhibited, the provision of labor power and raw materials required for the development of capitalist production will not be forthcoming, and that development will be stunted.

In sum, the transitional social formation is characterized by (1) the partial determination of prices by labor time, (2) a series of effects on the rent form as a result of the existence of capitalist production relations, and (3) a general class contradiction between feudal and capitalist relations of production.

THE TRANSITIONAL SOCIAL FORMATION AND UNDERDEVELOPMENT

At this point, the implications of the above for the study of modern day underdevelopment will be brought out. I have distinguished in earlier chapters between synchronic and diachronic analysis. The transitional social formation, as a framework, is the product of diachronic analysis; it consists in extending Marx's theory of the capitalist mode of production to social formations, which consist of more than one mode of production.

Within the concept of the transitional social formation, several possibilities exist. Conjunctures characterized by nondominance, where no mode of production has a sufficient degree of correspondence to dominate other social relations, may be analyzed. Examples of such nondominance, in addition to Bettelheim's analysis of the Soviet Union, include Latin America and the Caribbean prior to about 1940, although the transition occurred much later in certain Latin American and Caribbean countries, e.g., Peru.

Other conjunctures are more appropriately analyzed with reference to the framework discussed by Balibar, in which the specific action of the elements of the capitalist mode of production is to transform, sector by sector, the forces and relations of production. Under such conditions, the capitalist mode of production is said to be dominant, and virtually all of Latin America fits into this category today. However, some caveats are in order. This dominance can only be understood through an examination of the relations of production in a given conjuncture; it is not a simple implication of the dominance of capitalism at the world level. Second, even where a conjuncture is characterized by the dominance of one mode of production over another, there is no guarantee of transformation. That is, under certain circumstances and over an indefinite period, the recomposition of precapitalist relations may be the predominant tendency. Finally, the character of the transition to capitalist dominance will condition the development possibilities of the posttransition conjuncture.

As discussed above, the transitional social formation is characterized by two dislocations: a noncorrespondence between levels, i.e., between the relations of production and the legal forms taken by these relations, and a noncorrespondence between connections, i.e., between the relations and forces of production. These dislocations have important implications for the dynamics of underdevelopment.

The capitalist mode of production, described as a synchrony, does not possess such dislocations. On the contrary, the social relations of production are expressed in the form of economic calculation characteristic of capitalism, i.e., abstract labor takes the form of value. In addition, the forces of production (modern machinery) correspond to the social relations of production, which require the reproduction of the worker as a nonpossessor of the means of production.

The correspondence between connections requires the thorough mechanization of all sectors of production. The pace of this mechanization determines the rhythm of the cycles of reproduction. The possibility of reproduction is established by the relationship between the production of *Department I* goods and *Department II* goods. So long as the demand for *Department I* goods is sufficiently robust, the demand for *Department II* goods will meet supply, under certain assumptions about income distribution. Potential for disruption of the cycle lies in uneven mechanization, which can create sectoral imbalances and a crisis of disproportionality. Thus, smooth social reproduction is not guaranteed. Rather, reproduction takes place in uneven business cycles.

The other correspondence, that between the levels of the mode of production, relates to the fundamental tendency of the capitalist mode of production, the tendency of the rate of profit to fall. Because labor times are expressed as values, competition forces the introduction of technical progress and the piling up of value in the rising organic composition of capital. Unless this tendency is counteracted, a fall in the general profit rate will lead to a reduction in the demand for *Department I* goods and a crisis will break out. Note that the crisis originates in a failure to produce sufficient surplus value, though it will take the form of unrealized values.

Thus, in a synchrony, the correspondences determine a dynamic that reproduces the mode of production, albeit unevenly and through the equilibrating mechanism of crisis. The role of the state is to maintain the conditions for reproduction. State intervention in economic calculation arises either from the need to manipulate demand and thus affect the timing of the business cycle, or the need to establish practices at the level of social capital that individual capitalists could never undertake.

Similarly, the dislocations associated with a diachrony have implication for the laws of motion. Because the forces of production are not transformed in accordance with the social relations of production, the sectoral linkages discussed above do not exist. In the extreme, capitalist production in an isolated sector has neither the capital goods required for production nor a market for its product. In periods of manufacture this implies the persistence of feudal monopoly. In the context of the modern world economy, the diachronic analogue of the crisis of disproportionality is the balance of payments crisis, since *Department I* goods must be imported and paid for by exports. Since the relevant market is abroad, domestic production does not create demand and reproduction is not possible on the same basis as in a synchrony.

The noncorrespondence between levels is seen in the fact that only a portion of the value of labor power is produced in the capitalist sector. That is, precapitalist relations of production are expressed in capitalist economic calculation, but prices are not determined, even approximately, by labor time. Surplus value is produced only by absolute means. Thus, the overall profitability of capital is not determined by the production of value, since productivity may have little effect on the price of labor. Profitability will depend largely on demand that is external to the capitalist mode of production. Turning once again to modern-day underdevelopment, external demand will either be foreign or else will be demand for luxuries by the landlord class.

The latter case illustrates the fundamental form of class conflict in the transitional social formation. The maintenance of a landlord class, despite its inherent antagonism to the development of capitalism, may nevertheless provide a market for the capitalist sector. This contradiction played a role in the import substitution period in Latin America. Another example of structural ambivalence regarding the transformation of production relations concerns the production of wage goods. Wage goods are produced outside the capitalist sector, i.e., in the precapitalist sector (unless they are imported). Wage goods may be cheapened by transforming agricultural relations, but if such a solution is politically impossible they may also be cheapened by state intervention in the urban-rural terms of trade, i.e., by forcing the peasant to live below the subsistence level. The results of this policy, functional dualism and semi-proletarianization, have been analyzed by several authors.[7] In either case, the role of the state should be noted. In the capitalist mode of production as a synchrony, the state maintains the conditions of reproduction; in the transitional social formation, the state must play an active role in *establishing* the conditions of reproduction.[8]

INTERNAL AND EXTERNAL RELATIONS

These remarks have been meant to show the application of diachronic analysis to the question of underdevelopment, an application which, as mentioned in earlier chapters, has been explored by several writers. However, underdevelopment cannot be understood without some reference to the problematic of international relations. There are two broad questions to be answered in this context: (1) how was the present world division of labor, in which certain countries almost exclusively produce primary commodities, established, and (2) what is the dynamic of current North–South economic relations.

It is first necessary to understand that the concepts of synchrony and diachrony are not limited to an understanding of national economies. We have seen above that the tendency of the capitalist mode of production, the falling rate of profit and its countertendencies, becomes the transformation/recomposition struggle of the diachrony. Similarly, when this same tendency is viewed through the prism of international economic relations, it becomes surplus transfer. This is to say, in essence, that the transformation of the social relations in less developed countries will depend, in some measure, on the boom and bust rhythms of advanced capitalist countries and, specifically, on the immediacy of the need on the part of advanced capitalist countries to overcome the tendency of the rate of profit to fall.

To go beyond this, however, one must recognize that this struggle is highly conditioned by an existing world division of labor, a division of labor established as part of the transition to capitalism in Europe. This argument has been made forcefully by Geoffrey Kay.[9] As seen above, the transition to capitalism in Europe involved a differential development in the circuit of capital: merchant and productive capital. And, in general, the development of merchant capital is not sufficient to transform precapitalist production relations. In order to understand the role of merchant capital in establishing the basis for modern imperialism, we need to look more closely at its fundamental nature.

Capital, as value in motion, must accumulate to survive. The statement is no less true of merchant capital than of industrial capital. However, while productive capital extracts surplus value from the production process and exchanges commodities at their value, merchant capital profits from unequal exchange. The circuit of productive capital includes merchant capital, since goods must be sold to realize a profit, but merchant capital profits are a deduction from surplus value. The struggle implied by this contradiction was manifested in a political struggle between fractions of the capitalist class in Europe. The ultimate victory of industrial capital in Europe displaced this contradiction to the international level, where it raged throughout the development of capitalism in Europe and has played a determining role in what is today called underdevelopment.

Merchant capital, as circulation capital, requires the production of commodities but is indifferent to the mode of production. Hence, when circulation capital encounters noncapitalist modes of production, the effect has progressive and conservative aspects. The expansion of commodity production is a necessary condition for transformation, but this transformation is accomplished by merchant capital itself. On the contrary, " . . . the independent development of merchant capital . . . stands in inverse proportion to the general economic development of society."[10]

The full transition to capitalism in Europe required that the form, merchant capital, be overcome by capital in its general form, industrial capital. In England, intraclass rivalry ended in the political defeat of merchant capital. The repeal of the Corn Laws spelled the end of the state supported monopolies (a condition necessary for the supremacy of merchant capital) in Britain, and victory for free trade—hence, for industrial capital. Although merchant capital retained its power in the underdeveloped world, its role was altered by its defeat in the metropolis.

In the colonies, merchant capital found itself without the restrictions that its domestic dependence on industrial capital implied. The destructive effects of merchant capital in the colonies is well known. As Kay notes, "Merchant capital trades where it can and what it can, without concern or scruple: here slaves; there opium."[11] Whole civilizations were destroyed as a result.

Following its political defeat in Europe, merchant capital was still the only form of capital in the underdeveloped world, but now it began to operate as an aspect of metropolitan industrial capital. From the nineteenth century on, trade in the Third World takes on the familiar pattern of exported raw materials and food, as well as imported finished goods. The stage was thus set for modern imperialism. The tendency for merchant capital to inhibit the development of productive forces while developing trade continues into the twentieth century, but a second tendency appears: the tendency for underdeveloped economies to organize themselves around the needs of foreign industrial capital.

Therefore, while there are important similarities between the transition to capitalism in Europe and underdevelopment today, the nature of the transition in less developed countries is conditioned by (1) centuries of domination by independent merchant capital, (2) at least a century of domination by merchant capital as the special form of existence of industrial capital in the underdeveloped world, and (3) the ongoing imperialism associated with the export of capital itself.

The export of capital most closely reproduces the diachronic transformation/functionalization dynamic on the international stage. Capital in the center, in an effort to overcome the cyclical tendency for rate of profit to fall, seeks the higher profit rates available in the periphery. These profit rates are made possible by the combination of low wages (as a result of functional dualism) and high rates of productivity available to foreign investors. Surplus is thus transferred internationally in the form of interest payments on loans and repatriated profits from direct investment. However, the relationship between foreign control and precapitalist sectors is not fundamentally different from that between domestic capital and precapitalist sectors.

ACCUMULATION AND ECONOMIC CALCULATION IN THE TRANSITIONAL SOCIAL FORMATION

The transitional social formation is characterized by struggle between the classes defined by two sets of production relations. Each set of relations requires a certain transformation of the forces of production, and these forms of development are in contradiction. Feudal relations entail a decentralized development under the control of local landlords; this is in conflict with the capitalist centralization of the productive forces. Under conditions of capitalist dominance, the power of the landlords has been crushed and the peasantry functions as a survival. Nevertheless, the social relations associated with this survival have proven very resistant, in certain cases, to transformation.

The struggle takes place over the form in which surplus labor is to apear in the social formation. That is, a relation of mutual limitation exists between rent and profit, each limiting the expanded reproduction of antagonistic production relations. The rent relation, relying upon landlord control over a decentralized production process for its expansion, reduces capital's capacity to accumulate surplus labor in the form of profits by bringing a portion of social labor under its influence, that is, by limiting the quantity of surplus value available for accumulation. This limiting effect, however, is not a simple deduction from profit, but a restriction on the form in which capital can increase the quantity of surplus value produced by the working class. Similarly, capitalist production, implying commodity production in the first place and the circulation of labor power in the second, restricts the basis on which rent is produced; in other words, it restricts the reproduction of the tenant as a nonowning, agricultural producer. Thus, the struggle over the form of economic calculation is one over dominance in the social formation, in which the ruling class defined by each production relation attempts to establish the conditions under which those relations can be expanded in a less impeded manner.

We have seen in earlier chapters that the transitional social formation is characterized by noncorrespondence between forces and relations of production, as well as between production relations and the legal form of these relations. These dislocations exercise effects principally on the relation between agriculture and manufacture. The predominance of precapitalist relations of production in agriculture is sufficient to cast doubt on the generality of Smith's model of town-and-country cooperation. These relations are antagonistic to mechanization in agriculture, as Brenner has forcefully argued. In fact, the effect of rising demand for agricultural products, given commodity production, will be to reenforce feudal production relations and to reduce (or severely restrict) agricultural productivity. Thus, the existence of precapitalist relations in agriculture is reflected in the legal form of food prices, but these prices are determined by class struggle over the rent relation.[12] Consequently, wages, as well, express noncapitalist relations of production that are antagonistic to mechanization. The existence of these relations restricts increases in surplus value to absolute means. Moreover, the wage-profit relation is more complex in the transitional social formation than in the capitalist mode of production. For, in the former, a decrease in the rate of surplus value may indicate an increase in the power of landlords, as well as the presence of working-class resistance to capital.

To the extent that the capitalist class enjoys state power, it will extend credit in such a way as to allow price increases in sectors crucial to the development of the forces of production. Several points should be made, however, about capitalist state power. Nothing is implied as to the social groupings in control of the state apparatus (civilian or military, liberal or conservative). It is only necessary that the state perform certain economic functions, not that it initiate bourgeois democratic reforms.[13] Secondly, the question of the dominance of capital at the political level cannot be fully separated from the influence of world capitalism on the transitional social formation.[14] Finally, the correspondence of capitalist and landlord representation in the state will determine struggles over food prices, land reform, land taxes, and, in general, over the degree of intervention of the state in the economy.

A capitalist state will attempt to establish the conditions for the development of capitalism through the manipulation of price ratios, and in many other ways. Where dramatic changes in the production process (as in the case of technology transfer) result in a contradiction between this development of the forces of production and the pace of the transformation determined by the price structure as a reflection of feudal and capitalist relations of production, the state will attempt to resolve that contradiction by altering the structure of relative prices. Whether this action takes the form of price-fixing, subsidies, or selective credit policies depends upon a variety of economic, political, and ideological factors, but the effect is, in any case, upward price pressure in key sectors of production. These price increases will be sanctioned by an increase in the supply of money, and followed by increases in other prices, money wages, and rents.

It is important to recognize that there is nothing automatic about this process. It involves the intervention of a state, to the extent that it is capitalist in the sense suggested above, in the class struggle between landlords and capitalists. The effects of the struggle are most visible in the structure of relative prices and in changes in the absolute level of prices.

As we recall from earlier chapters, economic calculation in the capitalist mode of production is altered by state intervention in production, indirectly through state financial backing of centralization and concentration and, to a lesser extent, directly, as the state attempts to maintain the conditions necessary to reproduction. Recall also, however, that the inflationary effects of state-backed financing are negated entirely if the rate of accumulation that results from the credit-backed investment brings forth a total value of commodities equal to the money in circulation.

Otherwise, the inflation will bring about a deviation of wages from the value of labor power, raising the rate of surplus value. Real wages will fall unless the technical change resulting from the investment lowers the value of labor power to the new money wage. All of this is subject to the boom and bust rhythm of capitalist accumulation.

How are things different in the transitional social formation? First of all, the degree of state involvement is greater in the transitional social formation. To the extent that the state represents the local bourgeoisie, it will be actively involved in the struggle against both workers and classes thrown up by other social relations. Under certain conditions, as discussed below, the state will be leading the transformation of production relations.

In addition, the deviation of wages from the value of labor power is more problematic. The limits within which the wage can vary are more strict, in a fundamental sense, since the value of labor power may already be close to physical subsistence. This is not to deny that the ability of workers in a given conjuncture to resist these variations may also be very limited, but the degree of social disruption will be nonetheless greater.

Furthermore, and of greater importance, transitional social formations are characterized by a noncorrespondence between levels, i.e., noncapitalist relations are expressed in the capitalist ideological forms of prices and wages. This implies that technical progress will not significantly affect the value of labor power. Consequently, the increase in the rate of surplus value will mean an absolute decline in the living conditions of workers, as opposed to the relative impoverishment typical of the capitalist mode of production.

In addition to the noncorrespondence between levels, the property and real appropriation connections are disarticulated with respect to each other. Therefore, the development of the forces of production is uneven in the extreme. In some sectors, the market has the power to elicit a development of the productive forces, so that growth will be unbalanced. Specifically, the long-term response of agriculture supply will be very inelastic.

As a result, the terms of the trade-off between growth and inflation will be very harsh. This effect has been well developed by the structuralists and has led to the view that inflation is the price of growth in less developed countries.[15] As capital enters the growth sector, increasing employment bids up the price of food. Money wages rise in response and a spiral may occur. Moreover, " . . . the rate of increase in prices will be higher the greater the dispersion of demand, or productivity growth, between industries."[16]

The effect of rising demand for food on the agrarian sector, in general and over the long term, will be perverse. Landlords will raise money rents, and may try to raise output by coercing tenants to increase their surplus labor through absolute means, but without productivity increases the long-term effect will be to exhaust the land and reduce output.

The state committed to the development of capitalism can try to find relief in agricultural policy. The type of policy chosen will depend on the fraction of capital with state power, the resistance of the precapitalist relations, and the conjunctural history of the state and its relation to the agrarian classes. Roughly speaking, however, two roads lay open. The state can set about to turn the terms of trade against agriculture or it can attempt to induce a transformation of production relations in that sector.

The popularity of agricultural price manipulation by the state is evidence of the functional dualism of precapitalist relations. Were the state to attempt to coerce capitalist farmers into increasing the agricultural surplus by *lowering* food prices, capital would shift out of agriculture and less efficient producers would be eliminated. Nonspecialized peasants can be coerced, however, either directly by the state or by landlords, because they will increase effort, providing the surplus at lower prices, or even increasing the surplus in an attempt to maintain the same revenue. The alternative is the loss of land.

In the alternative, the state can attempt to induce an agrarian transition, i.e., to stimulate the growth of capitalism in the countryside by selective subsidies and other means.

Finally, the state can embark upon a stabilization plan, either in conjunction with agriculture policy or without it. Typically, the program will combine fiscal conservatism with an incomes policy to reduce real wages.

By way of example, the Brazilian state has tried all three policies. A series of developmentalist administrations pursued a policy of urban bias without any real attempt at transformation from the end of World War II until the military coup of 1964. During this period, the power of the traditional landholding classes in the export sector was broken, and capitalist dominance was established. Through control of the state, the urban bourgeoisie established policies with a bias against agriculture. Prior to 1953, the principal plank of this policy was an overvalued cruzeiro. In later years, more direct pricing policies served to keep the internal price of agriculture below the world price, subsidizing the value of labor power.[17] This agricultural policy was pursued along with inflationary finance of infrastructual investments, and production of domestic industry.

While this policy weakened the landlord class and reduced short-term inflationary pressures, it did little to hasten the growth of capitalism in Brazilian agriculture. By the late 1950s, the terms of trade had begun to shift in favor of agriculture. The subsequent distributional struggle led to the 1964 military coup and subsequent stabilization policy. Over the next several years, the military set a minimum wage constrained to lag behind the growth in prices, crushed the trade unions, and restricted the extension of credit. The "miracle" began in 1968, but by 1974 the growth rate had fallen and rising food prices had once again begun an inflationary spiral. As a consequence, the government launched an aggressive agrarian program designed to bring about a capitalist transformation in agriculture without land redistribution, i.e., to convert large holdings into large agribusinesses, by means of massive capital equipment subsidies.

In the transitional social formation, economic calculation is an expression of a complex class struggle both within the capitalist class and between the capitalist and precapitalist classes. The effects of this struggle on the possibilities for growth have been outlined in this section.

CONCLUSION

This chapter has developed the concept of the transitional social formation in order to explain underdevelopment. Of particular importance is the concept of economic calculation in the transitional social formation. The principal conclusion is that noncorrespondence between levels and connections characterize the transitional social formation. This has specific implications for the phenomenon of underdevelopment, and for accumulation in less developed countries.

NOTES

1. Bettelheim, *Economic Calculation*, p. 71.
2. Hindess and Hirst, *Pre-Capitalist Modes of Production*, pp. 255–59.
3. Ronald Meek, *Smith, Marx, & After* (London: Chapman & Hall, 1977), pp. 134–45.
4. Marx, *Capital*, 3:671.
5. I distinguish between feudal and modern monopoly in the following section. However, it must already be clear that while feudal monopoly rests upon an inhibition on the capitalist development of the forces of production, modern monopoly is a result of this development.
6. In the present day, such a conflict is seen in the struggle over conflicting development policies, such as "export promotion" versus "import substitution."
7. See, especially, de Janvry, *The Agrarian Question and Reformism in Latin America*, pp. 81–93.
8. C. Thomas, *The Rise of the Authoritarian State in Peripheral Societies* (New York: Monthly Review Press, 1984).
9. G. Kay, *Development and Underdevelopment: A Marxist Analysis* (London: Macmillan, 1975).
10. *Capital*, Vol. III, p. 328.
11. Kay, p. 101.
12. It is more precise to say that food prices are overdetermined, first of all, because the level of productivity in the urban sector will exercise some effect on these prices, if in no other way than through its effect on the cost of distribution, and secondly, because political intervention by a capitalist state may involve altering the level of food prices.
13. Capital does not always exercise state power in its own name, as Marx demonstrated in *The Eighteenth Brumaire of Louis Bonaparte* (Moscow: Foreign Languages Publishing House, 1959).

14. Fernandez makes this point very well, see p. 43.

15. The structuralist theory of inflation, as well as other theories of inflation, are discussed in K. Perkins, *Inflation in the Context of Development*, Unpublished Dissertation, May 1982, The American University, Washington, D.C.

16. A. P. Thirlwall, *Inflation, Saving and Growth in Developing Economies* (New York: St. Martin's, 1974), p. 54.

17. Goodman and Redclift, *From Peasant to Proletarian*, pp. 128–84.

13

CONCLUSION

In writing this book, my central desire has been to show that the theoretical problems associated with underdevelopment can be rendered more tractable by considering them in relation to the transition to capitalism. Toward this end, I have examined Balibar's general theory of modes of production in some detail. This theory is derived by generalizing certain of the procedures employed by classical political economists in their analyses of the capitalist mode of production, and applying them to other modes of production. As I have argued above, the creation of a theoretical space in which different modes of production can be situated is a prerequisite for a theory of transition. We have seen that, in attempts to understand the transition as a phase of precapitalist or capitalist development, as an object of knowledge it disappears from view. For this reason, I am in broad agreement with Balibar's approach.

On the other hand, as seen above, Balibar's transitional mode of production is too rigidly restricted to the analysis of the dominance of one mode of production over others. Consequently, I have followed Bettelheim in the employment of the concept of a transitional social formation, a concept which I have developed over several chapters. As a matter of fact, however, I have found several of the concepts developed by Balibar in his discussion of the transitional mode of production, notably the concept of noncorrespondence, to be very useful in the construction of the transitional social formation.

A further generalization from the analysis of capitalism is the notion of a general theory of economic calculation, or a theory of the forms taken by social labor in different modes of production. I have employed this concept in the following manner. I sought the form of economic calculation, first, characteristic of the capitalist mode of production, and then, the form characteristic of the feudal mode of production. Of particular importance was the designification to which the economic calculation characteristic of a particular mode of production is subject. We also saw that feudal production relations determine a specific transformation of the productive forces. This left the way clear for an analysis of economic calculation in the transitional social formation. Here, the forms of economic calculation place limits upon each other. The existence of the rent relation, for example, limits the surplus value available for the expansion of the circuits of capital, while the existence of the wage-labor relation threatens the reproduction of the rent relation, specifically by inhibiting the reproduction of the tenant as a nonowning, agricultural producer. I have opposed the operation of the transitional social formation to the rosier scenarios of Sweezy and Rey, in which capitalism and feudalism cooperate to create the conditions for capitalist development.

I began the book with a discussion of the "development of underdevelopment" school. I have argued, throughout this book, that it is not necessary to lose sight of the production relations at play in a social formation in order to explain either the internal or the external relations of less developed countries. After a brief introduction to French "Structuralism," I reviewed some recent literature on accumulation and crisis in advanced capitalism. In particular, I examined the monetary role of the state in the deviation of prices from values, and the necessity for this intervention, as well as the limits to its success.

In several chapters on diachronic analysis, I developed the concept of the transitional social formation. In the course of this development, I critiqued the "commercialization" model of transition, and developed a general concept of economic calculation that can be applied to different modes of production. Finally, I applied the concept of the transitional social formation to the phenomenon of underdevelopment. Of particular interest here is the application of the notion of the dislocations associated with the transitional social formation to the condition of less developed countries. Many of the stylized facts of underdevelopment turn out to be aspects of these dislocations. These dislocations have special implications for the formation of prices, urban/rural terms of trade, and the role of the state.

I close by mentioning two directions in which further research is indicated. First of all, class struggle in the transitional social formation appears as an interpenetration of economic calculations, forms of calculation that mutually limit each other. And, I have argued that control over the state is a key aspect of this struggle, since the state influences the formation of prices. However, I have not specified the relationship between the struggle of two ruling classes over dominance in the social formation and the struggle among the myriad class factions, with or without some form of representation in the state, which typify social struggles in developing social formations. Clearly, the specification of this relationship calls for analysis at a more concrete level, bringing into account aspects from which I have abstracted in this book.

A second set of problems upon which the concepts of economic calculation and of the transitional social formation may shed light is related to the internationalization of the law of value. As we have seen, a variety of theories of surplus extraction through international prices assume that all countries are capitalist (e.g., Emmanuel). If this is not the case, then the value of a commodity with an international price is problematized. The central question is: what relations of production does such a (international) law of value tend to reproduce?

Once again, I hope that this work will encourage creative research in the theory and practice of economic development. There are few areas of research on the contemporary scene that are as fascinating, or as pressing.

SELECTED BIBLIOGRAPHY

Althusser, Louis. *For Marx*. London: New Left Books, 1977.

————. *Lenin and Philosophy and Other Essays*. London: New Left Books, 1971.

Althusser, Louis, and Balibar, Etienne. *Reading Capital*. Translated by Ben Brewster. London: New Left Books, 1977.

Amin, Samir. *Accumulation on a World Scale*. New York: Monthly Review Press, 1968.

Anderson, Perry. *Arguments Within English Marxism*. New York: Monthly Review Press, 1968.

Banaji, J. "Modes of Production in a Materialist Conception of History." *Capital and Class*. Vol. 3 (Autumn 1977).

Baran, Paul. *The Political Economy of Growth*. New York: Monthly Review Press, 1968.

Barkin, David, and Esteva, Gustavo. "Social Conflict and Inflation in Mexico." *Latin American Perspectives*. No. 33 (Winter 1982), pp. 48–64.

Beckford, George L. *Persistent Poverty: Underdevelopment in the Plantation Regions of the World*. New York: Oxford University Press, 1971.

Beckford, George, and Witter, Michael. *Small Garden . . . Bitter Weed: Struggle and Change in Jamaica*. London: Zed Press, 1982.

Bernal, Richard. "Resolving the Debt Crisis." U.W.I. Monograph #1. Kingston, Jamaica: 1985.

Blair, John. "Market Power and Inflation: A Short-Run Target Return Model." *Journal of Economic Issues* (June 1974): 453–77.

Bettelheim, Charles. *Economic Calculation and Forms of Property*. London: Routledge and Kegan Paul, 1976.

Brenner, Robert. "Agrarian Class Structure and Economic Development in Pre-industrial Europe." *Past and Present*. No. 70 (February 1976), pp. 35–75.

————. "The Origins of Capitalist Development: A Critique of Neo-Smithian Marxism." *New Left Review*. No. 104 (July/August 1977), pp. 25–92.

Brewer, Anthony. *Marxist Theories of Imperialism, A Critical Survey*. London: Routledge & Kegan Paul, 1980.

Brunhoff, Suzanne de. *Les rapports d'argent*. Grenoble: Presses Universitaires de Grenoble, 1979.

Callinicos, Alex. *Althusser's Marxism*. London: Pluto Press, 1976.

Colletti, Lucio. "A Political and Philosophical Interview." *New Left Review*. No. 86 (1978), pp. 8–41.

————. "Comments on Marx's Theory of Value." *The Subtle Anatomy of Capitalism*. Edited by Jesse Schwartz. Santa Monica, California: Goodyear Publishing Co., 1977, pp. 458–73.

————. *Marxism and Hegel*. London: New Left Books, 1973.

Consequegra, Jose. *Un nuevo enfogue de la teoria de la inflacion*. Bogota: Ediciones Tercer Mundo, 1976.

Dallemagne, Jean-Luc. "L'inflation et crisis ou le mythe de la 'stagflation.' " In *Critique de l'economie politique*, pp. 156–86. Paris: Francois Maspero, 1974.

Dore, Elizabeth, and Weeks, John. "International Exchange and the Causes of Backwardness." Washington, D.C., 1979 Unpublished paper.

Dobb, Maurice. *Studies in the Development of Capitalism*. New York: International Publishers, 1963.

Economic Commission for Latin America. *Development Problems in Latin America*. Austin: University of Texas Press, 1969.

Emmanuel, Arghiri. *Unequal Exchange, A Study of the Imperialism of Trade*. With theoretical comments by Charles Bettelheim. Translated by Brian Pearce. New York: Monthly Review Press, 1972.

Engels, Friedrich. *Anti-Duhring*. Moscow: Foreign Language Publishing House, 1962.

————. *Dialetics of Nature*. Moscow: International Publishers, 1954.

Felix, David. "An Alternative View of the 'Monetarist'-'Structuralist' Controversy." In *Latin American Issues, Essays and Comments*, pp. 81–93. Edited by Albert O. Hirschman. New York: The Twentieth Century Fund, 1961.

Fernandez, Raul. "Imperialist Capitalism in the Third World: Theory and Evidence from Colombia." *Latin American Perspectives*. No. 79 (Winter 1979), pp. 38–64.

Feyerabend, Paul. *Against Method*. Atlantic Highlands, New Jersey: Humanities Press, 1975.

Fine, Ben, and Harris, Laurence. *Rereading Capital*. New York: Columbia University Press, 1979.

Foster-Carter, Alain. "The Modes of Production Controversy." *New Left Review*. No. 107 (January–February 1978).

Furtado, Celso. *Economic Development of Latin America*. 2nd edition. Cambridge: Cambridge University Press, 1976.

Frank, André Gunder. *Latin America: Underdevelopment or Revolution*. New York: Monthly Review Press, 1969.

Girvan, Norman. "Notes on Jamaica's External Debt." U.W.I. Monograph. Kingston, Jamaica: 1985.

Glyn, Andrew, and Sutcliffe, Robert. *British Capital, Workers and the Profit Squeeze*. London: Penguin, 1972.

Glucksmann, André. "A Ventriloquist Structuralism." *New Left Review*. No. 72 (March–April 1972), pp. 100–60.

Godelier, Maurice. "Infrastructures, Societies and History." *New Left Review*. No. 112 (November–December 1978), pp. 84–96.

———. *Perspectives in Marxist Anthropology*. Translated by Robert Brain. Cambridge: Cambridge University Press, 1977.

Goodman, David and Michael Redclift. *From Peasant to Proletarian: Capitalist Development and Agrarian Transitions*. New York: St. Martin's Press, 1982.

Hart, Keith. *The Political Economy of West African Agriculture*. Cambridge: Cambridge University Press, 1982.

Harris, Laurence. "On Interest, Credit and Capital." *Economy and Society*. No. 15 (May 1976): 145–77.

Harvey, J. "Theories of Inflation." *Marxism Today*. 21 (January 1977): 24–28.

Hilferding, Rudolph. *Finance Capital*. Boston: Routledge & Kegan Paul, 1981.

Hilton, Rodney., ed. *The Transition from Feudalism to Capitalism*. London: New Left Books, 1976; Verso edition, 1978.

Himmelweit, Susan, and Mohun, Simon. "The Anomalies of Capital." *Capital and Class*. No. 6 (August 1978), pp. 67–105.

Hindess, Barry, and Hirst, Paul. *Pre-Capitalist Modes of Production*. London: Routledge and Kegan Paul, 1975.

Janvry, Alain de. *The Agrarian Question and Reformism in Latin America*. Baltimore: Johns Hopkins, 1981.

Jones, Gareth Steedman. "Engels and the End of Classical German Philosophy." *New Left Review*. No. 79 (May–June 1973), pp. 8–26.

Kay, G. *Development and Underdevelopment: A Marxist Analysis*. London: Macmillan, 1975.

Keat, Russell, and Urry, John. *Social Theory as Science*. London: Routledge and Kegan Paul, 1975.

Koshimura, S. *Theory of Capital Reproduction and Accumulation*. Edited by Jesse Schwartz. Translated by Toshihira Ataka. Kitchener, Canada: DPG Publishing Co., 1975.

Laclau, Ernesto. "Feudalism and Capitalism in Latin America." *New Left Review*. No. 67 (1971).

Lenin, V. I. *The Development of Capitalism in Russia*. Moscow: Progress Publishers, 1964.

Lukacs, Georg. *History of Class Consciousness*. London: Camelot Press, 1971.

Mandel, Ernest. *Late Capitalism*. London: New Left Books, 1975.

Marini, Ruy. *La dialectica de la dependencia*. Mexico City: Ediciones Era, 1975.

Marx, Karl. *Capital, A Critique of Political Economy*. 3 vols. Edited by Friedrich Engels. New York: International Publishers, 1967.

———. *The Eighteenth Brumaire of Louis Bonaparte*. Moscow: Foreign Languages Publishing House, 1959.

———. *Grundrisse, Foundations of the Critique of Political Economy*. New York: Vintage Books, 1973.

————. *Pre-Capitalist Economic Formations*. London: Lawrence and Wishart, 1964.

Marx, Karl, and Engels, Friedrich. *The German Ideology*. London: International Publishers, 1970.

Mattick, Paul. *Economics, Politics, and the Age of Inflation*. White Plains, New York: M. E. Sharpe Inc., 1978.

Meek, Ronald. *Smith, Marx, & After*. London: Chapman & Hall, 1977.

Meillassoux, Claude. *Antropologie economique des Gouro de Côte-d'Ivoire*. Paris: Mouton, 1964.

Perkins, Katherine. *Inflation in the Context of Development*. Washington, D.C.: American University Doctoral Dissertation, 1982.

————. "Food Crisis and Agricultural Policy in the Caribbean." Unpublished paper presented at the Caribbean Studies Association Conference, Kingston, Jamaica: May 1982.

————. "One Dey, One Dey, Con Go Tey: An Analysis of the Grenadian Revolution." Unpublished paper presented at the Caribbean Studies Association Conference, St. Kitts and Nevis: May 1984.

Postan, M. M. *The Medieval Economy and Society: an Economic History of Britain: 1100–1500*. Berkeley: University of California Press, 1972.

Purton, John. "Inflation and the Working Class." *Marxism Today* 18 (January 1974): 20–28.

Rey, Pierre-Philippe. *Colonialisme, neo-colonialisme et transition au capitalisme*. Paris: Francois Maspero, 1971.

————. *Les alliances des classes*. Paris: Francois Maspero, 1976.

Robinson, Joan. *Economic Philosophy*. Chicago: Aldine Publishing Company, 1962.

Rodney, Walter. *How Europe Underdeveloped Africa*. Dar es Saalam and London: Tanzania Publishing House and Bogle L'Ouverture Publications, 1972.

Seton, Francis. "The Transformation Problem." *Review of Economic Studies* 24 (1957): 149–60.

Sherman, Howard. "Inflation, Unemployment and Monopoly Capitalism." *Monthly Review* 27 (1975): 25–35.

Smith, Adam. *An Inquiry Into the Nature and Causes of the Wealth of Nations*. New York: Random House, Inc., 1937.

Steedman, Ian. *Marx After Sraffa*. London: New Left Books, 1977.

Sunkel, Osvaldo. "Un esquema general para el analisis de la inflacion." *Economia*. No. 62 (1959), pp. 72–118.

Sweezy, Paul. "Varieties of Inflation." *Monthly Review* 30 (1978): 44–49.

Terray, E. *Marxism and Primitive Societies, Two Studies*. New York: Monthly Review Press, 1972.

Therborn, Goran. *Science, Class, and Society*. London: New Left Books, 1976.

Thirlwall, A. P. *Inflation, Saving and Growth in Developing Economies*. New York: St. Martin's, 1974.

Thomas, Clive. *Dependence and Transformation: The Economics of the Transition to Socialism*. New York and London: Monthly Review Press, 1974.

————. *The Rise of the Authoritarian State in Peripheral Societies*. New York: Monthly Review Press, 1984.

Thompson, Edward. *The Poverty of Theory*. London: New Left Books, 1978.

Wallerstein, Immanuel. *The Modern World-System: Capitalist Agriculture and the Origins of the European World Economy in the Sixteenth Century.* New York: Academic Press, 1974.

Weeks, John. *Capital and Exploitation.* Princeton, New Jersey: Princeton University Press, 1981.

Williams, Eric. *Capitalism and Slavery.* London: André Deutsch, 1964.

Yaffe, David. "The Crisis of Profitability, A Critique of the Glyn-Sutcliffe Thesis." *New Left Review.* No. 80 (1973), pp. 40–49.

INDEX

Accumulation: capitalism and, 62-64, 95; commodity exchange and, 40; credit and, 44-45; gold sales and, 42; hoarding and, 44; inflation and, 45; in monopolies, 49; primitive, 12, 61-64, 84, 93, 98; production forces and, 58, 63, 95; rent and, 127; state-backed financing and, 128; synchronic analysis of, 39, 50-53; theories of, 39-45

Africa, modes of production in, 27

Agriculture: capitalism and, 10-12, 84, 96-102; commercialization and, 101-102; commoditization of, 12; mechanization in, 127; monocrop, 5; peasant labor and, 11; prices of, 5, 7; production relations in, 127, 129; productivity and, 101, 127; subsistence, 84

Althusser, Louis, 17-30, 32, 33, 68, 87

Amin, Samir, 9

Anti-Duhring (Engels), 19

Appropriation, 21, 24, 58, 68, 109

Aristotle, 21

Artisans, vs. collective workers, 59

Balance of payments, 5, 6, 8, 123

Balibar, Etienne, 21, 24-27, 28, 32-34, 55-59, 61-71, 73-75, 76, 79, 81, 82-83, 85, 108-109, 122, 133

Banaji, J., 12, 83

Baran, Paul, 8

Bentham, Jeremy, 20, 87

Bettelheim, Charles, 24, 26-27, 32-34, 55, 56-57, 76-77, 80, 84, 108-109, 122, 133

Bourgeoisie, 18, 33

Brazil, capitalism in, 130-131

Brenner, Robert, 93, 111, 113, 127, 100-103

Business cycles, 123

Callinicos, Alex, 23, 24

Capital (Marx), 32, 33, 86, 88, 110

Capitalism, 39-45; accumulation and, 62-64, 95; agricultural development and, 10-12, 84, 96-102; in Brazil, 130-131; class struggles and, 11, 107-110; commodities and, 27, 86, 101; contradictions in, 64-66; credit and, 42-44, 89, 127; cycles in, 85-86, 123-125; economic methods and, 39, 41, 76-78, 107-110, 122-123, 128, 133-134; in England, 17, 32, 125; fetishism in, 21, 30, 75-76; feudalism and, 27, 85-86, 98, 100-103; his-

Inflation: accumulation and, 45; capitalism and, 52; commodities and, 42; credit and, 42-44, 49-50; exports and, 6; food supply and, 5; gold value and, 42; hoarding and, 52; import controls and, 5-6; money policies and, 5; monopolies and, 7-8; obstructed development and, 4; profit repatriation and, 8; social formations and, 129; state financing and, 42-43, 128; wages and, 50, 128. *See also* Money
Infrastructure, economic, 28-29
Institutions, social reproduction and, 28
Interest, profits and, 49-52
International Monetary Fund, 4

de Janvry, Alain, 84
Juridical relations, 87

Kant, Immanuel, 23, 68
Kay, Geoffrey, 125
Khrushchev, N., 18
Knowledge, 19, 23
Kulak class, 11

Labor: adaptation of, 109; capitalism and, 25, 29, 31, 57-59, 66, 86-87, 110, 123; centralization and, 50-51, 53; as commodity, 29-30, 40, 86; exploitation of, 47; full employment of, 43, 50; homogenous, 7, 88; inflation and, 128; mechanization and, 25, 29, 59; mobility of, 104; prices and, 48-51, 109, 119-120; production forces and, 82; as rent, 31, 85-86, 96, 102, 112-113, 127; social division of, 20-21; socialization of, 44, 49, 58-59, 109; socially necessary, 111, 114; subsumption of, 55-59, 66, 114; unions and, 48; value theory and, 12, 41, 84-88, 123, 129. *See also* Production; Surplus labor; Wages
Laclau, Ernest, 12
Land, irrational price of, 89
Latin America, 4, 122, 124

Legal contracts, 29, 55-57
Lenin, Vladimir, 11, 21, 26
Lenin and Philosophy and Other Essays (Althusser), 24
Less developed countries: class relations in, 10; inflation and, 7; Marxism and, 18; monopoly in, 7-8; precapitalist relations and, 10-12; price of growth in, 129; production relations in, 10; progressive bourgeoisie in, 18; protectionism in, 4; social relations in, 124; transitions in, 126. *See also* Underdevelopment
Linear relations, 21-23
Lukacs, Georg, 19

Mandel, Ernest, 50
Manufacturing: as dislocation, 66, 81, 118; feudal production and, 96; industry and, 58-59; transition of, 56
Marini, Ruy, 8
Market theory, 9, 33, 50, 96-98, 102
Marx, Karl, 10, 69, 76, 107, 109-110; on accumulation, 61, 93, 94; bourgeois critics of, 28; on capital, 39-40; classical theory and, 67, 86-88; on competition, 51; economic determination and, 28; empiricism and, 33-34; exchange and, 39-40; humanism and, 87; labor value and, 84-88; market price and, 50; metalist theories and, 7; money theory, 7, 41-42; on precapitalist relations, 11, 30-32, 63, 94; production forces and, 10-11, 20; proletarian philosophy and, 24; on rent, 98-99; socialized labor and, 58-59; transformation procedure of, 48; on transition to capitalism, 11, 61-71; value production and, 40-45
Marxism: Althusser and, 18-30; feudalism and, 30-32; historicism and, 18-19; ideology and, 94-96; international workers' movement and, 18; in less developed countries, 18; scientific basis for, 20-21, 23-24, 27; societal structure and, 21-22; value

Prices (*continued*)
  tions and, 57, 89, 117; unions and,
  48; value and, 41-44, 79
Production, means of: agrarian reform
  and, 12; capitalism and, 11, 31, 66,
  108-109; causal relations and, 69-70,
  83; class struggles and, 23, 27, 69,
  80, 95-96, 98, 107-108, 110-115; contradictions and, 64-66, 96, 103, 117;
  control over, 113-114; direct producers and, 85-86, 104; dislocations
  in, 89, 119; economic methods and,
  75-78, 85-86, 107-115; forces in, 29,
  82-83, 95-96, 100; foreign ownership, 8; intellectual labor and, 59;
  labor socialization and, 27, 32-34,
  44, 77, 88; legal forms of, 29, 55-57;
  markets and, 79-80, 97-98, 102;
  mechanization and, 108, 120; noncorrespondence and, 55-57; politics
  and, 114; precapitalist, 63, 83, 88,
  97-98; prices and, 41, 50, 79-80, 89,
  119-120; property and, 56; relations
  in, 11, 25, 29-30, 81-83, 95-96, 98,
  100, 107-109, 115; reproduction in,
  62, 67, 99-100, 122-123; science in,
  66; social structure and, 21, 68-69,
  79-81, 99-100, 109, 117, 126-131;
  state intervention in, 121, 128;
  structure of, 61-71, 87; surplus
  value and, 9, 73; synchronic analysis of, 61. *See also* Productivity;
  specific sectors, types
Productivity: agriculture and, 101,
  127; credit and, 51-52; exploitation
  and, 47, 111-114; feudalism and, 95-
  97, 100, 102, 103-105, 111-114; increases in, 97, 100; labor value and,
  102, 123; liberation and, 97; mechanization and, 113; prices and, 89,
  123; rent and, 97, 102; surplus value
  and, 107; trade and, 102. *See also*
  Production, means of
Profits: capitalism and, 40-41, 43-44,
  64, 123-124, 126; class struggles
  and, 108; declines in, 123-124, 126;
  in feudalism, 118; mechanization
  and, 120; merchant capital and, 125;

monopolies and, 48, 51-52; in periphery, 126; prices and, 8, 50; production value and, 123; rent and,
  121, 127; repatriation of, 8, 126;
  state intervention in, 43-44; surplus
  value and, 47-48; technology and,
  51; unions and, 48; wages and, 8,
  48-50. *See also* Money
Proletarians, 19, 24
Property: capitalism and, 29, 56-57;
  feudalism and, 110; legal expression
  of, 56; modes of production and,
  24, 31; production and, 24, 31, 113;
  social formations and, 129; socialism and, 56-57
Protectionism, 4, 89

Reading Capital (Althusser and Balibar), 26, 32
Recessions, 44, 50
Rents: absolute, 98; class struggles
  and, 111; in capitalism, 112; in feudalism, 30, 103-105, 112; labor as,
  31, 85-86, 96, 102, 112-113, 127;
  Marx on, 98-99; money as, 31, 112,
  119, 121; peasant expropriation and,
  96-97, 100; productivity increases
  and, 31, 97; profits and, 121; social
  formations and, 98-99; trade and,
  102
Rey, Pierre-Phillipe, 12, 24, 27, 89,
  93, 97-100, 102, 117, 121
Ricardo, David, 77
Roman law, 56
Russia, 18, 21

Scientific method, 20-23, 66, 68, 96-97
Seigneurial domination, 85
Serfdom. *See* Peasants
Sherman, Howard, 49
Smith, Adam, 101, 127
Socialism: class struggles and, 81;
  commodity relations and, 27; prop-
  erty forms and, 56-57; social change
  and, 19; transition to, 26-27, 108;
  underdeveloped countries and, 6.
  See also Marxism; *specific con-
  cepts, doctrines*

ABOUT THE AUTHOR

M. KATHERINE PERKINS is an internationally known development economist. She has written extensively on the Caribbean and Latin America. In addition to development theory, her research focuses on issues in the areas of international trade and finance.

Among Dr. Perkins articles and papers are "An Economic Analysis of U.S. Drug Control Policy: The Impact on the Cannabis Trade," "The Dynamics of the Illicit Drug Trade and U.S. Policy in Latin America and the Caribbean," "The Food Crisis Economy: A Case Study of Jamaica," and "The Impact of Out-Migration on Agriculture in Small Island Economies: The Case of Grenada."

She is currently writing a second volume that is an application of the theories presented in this volume to concrete problems confronting countries in Latin America and the Caribbean today. She is also completing a book entitled *The Political Economy of the Illicit Drug Trade*.

Dr. Perkins is a graduate professor in the Department of Economics at Howard University in Washington, D.C., where she has been lecturing in the areas of international trade and development since 1981. In addition, she has taught at the University of Paris in France, and at the University of the West Indies in Jamaica, where she also served as a Visiting Research Scholar at the Institute for Social and Economic Research.